Presumption and the Practices of Tentative Cognition

NICHOLAS RESCHER
University of Pittsburgh

CAMBRIDGE
UNIVERSITY PRESS

CAMBRIDGE UNIVERSITY PRESS
Cambridge, New York, Melbourne, Madrid, Cape Town, Singapore, São Paulo

Cambridge University Press
40 West 20th Street, New York, NY 10011-4211, USA

www.cambridge.org
Information on this title: www.cambridge.org/9780521864749

© Nicholas Rescher 2006

First published 2006

Printed in the United States of America

A catalog record for this publication is available from the British Library.

Library of Congress Cataloging in Publication Data
Rescher, Nicholas.
Presumption and the practices of tentative cognition / Nicholas Rescher.
p.   cm.
Includes bibliographical references and index.
ISBN 0-521-86474-7 (hardback)
1. Hypothesis.   I. Title.
BC183.R42   2006
121′.6–dc22   2005031159

ISBN-13   978-0-521-86474-9 hardback
ISBN-10   0-521-86474-7 hardback

For Timo Airaksinen
in cordial friendship

Contents

Preface

"Dr. Livingston, I presume" runs the famous exclamation with which H. M. Stanley greeted the long-lost explorer. And in saying this he as much as said that "this is what I am going to take to be the case unless and until further developments should show that it is not." That is just exactly how presumption works.

The topic of presumption encompasses a wide range of practices within our quest for informative knowledge and practical decision. These particular resolutions, however, have a tentative quality in being taken to hold not with categorical assurance but rather provisionally and pro tem until such a point when (if ever) sufficiently strong counterindications come to light. Such presumptions carry a burden of proof that inclines upon anyone who is disinclined to accept them.

The practice of presumption arose initially in the law but subsequently became operative in virtually every area of rational endeavor, for presumption is a remarkably versatile and pervasively useful resource. Firmly grounded in the law of evidence from its origins in classical antiquity, it made its way in the days of medieval scholasticism into the theory and practice of disputation and debate. And it subsequently extended its reach to play an increasingly significant role in the philosophical theory of knowledge. It has thus come to represent a region where lawyers, debaters, and philosophers can all find some common ground.

This book has been conceived and written in the conviction that the epistemology of what might be called the lesser degrees of cognitive warrant is an area of considerable promise and potential. For there is good reason to think that this domain of the "inferior" generally discounted grades of knowledge is indispensable for an adequate theory of knowledge. And, as this book will endeavor to make abundantly clear, this is particularly the case with those low-grade data that may be characterized as *presumptions*. Unfortunately, however, their foothold in epistemology is still rather insecure, and it is the author's hope that this book will contribute toward remedying this shortcoming. For as this book's deliberations endeavor to show, the process of presumption plays a role of virtually indispensable utility in matters of rational inquiry and communication. The origin of presumption may lie in the law but its future is assured by its service to the theory of information management and the philosophy of science.

Chapter 1 sets the historical stage. Chapter 2 coordinates presumption with burden of proof. Chapters 3–4 explore the theme of cognitive presumption that amounts to policies, deemed effective in gaining knowledge: practical policies (with pragmatic justifications) that we tentatively accept, faute de mieux, in order to progress in our thinking. Chapter 5 continues the argument for pragmatic justification of presumption, situating it in our ongoing choice between accepting points about which we are not certain or alternatively accepting a skepticism that admits defeat. Chapter 6 is devoted to presumption in default reasoning and Chapters 7–8 explore its role in making sense of what is left unsaid. Chapter 9 is devoted to presumption in sciences such as physics. One presumption in a natural science such as physics is explored in Chapter 10 – namely, that specific information (as in an experimental observation) generally overrules a general hypothesis. Chapter 11 focuses on a very special case of presumption in our planning for the future, which in some cases dismisses extremely rare possibilities from the reckoning on the basis of what, in effect, are "judgment calls."

The range of issues that join together under the rubric of presumption collectively captures some of the complications and unkindness of our efforts to be rational and reasonable. For in the end these are not matters of mere logic alone but of a broadly "economic" striving to make the most effective possible use of our resources to meet the demands imposed by our needs.

Historically, the tendency of work in epistemology since Descartes has focused on certain knowledge, creating a tradition that ignores or at best slights the kinds of provisional and conjectural focus of epistemic endorsement on whose basis both our theorizing and our acting in the world generally proceed. Attention to the role of presumption in inquiry counteracts this tendency and reveals the inadequacy of fundamentalist epistemologies to provide alike a faithful departure of the practice of human inquiry and a cogent theoretical validation for its proceedings.

I am grateful to Estelle Burris for her help in preparing my manuscript for publication.

Pittsburgh, Pennsylvania
May 2005

Presumption and the Practices of Tentative Cognition

1

The Legal Roots of Presumption

1. What Presumption Is All About

To *presume* in the presently relevant sense of the term is to accept something in the absence of the further relevant information that would ordinarily be deemed necessary to establish it. The term derives from the Latin *praesumere*: to take before or to take for granted.[1] Presumption has figured in legal reasoning since classical antiquity. There is nothing modern or cutting-edge about it: it is one of the oldest tricks in the book.

Presumption found its first and still most prominent role in the context of the law, where a presumption mandates a trier to accept a certain fact once some other correlative fact has been established. The French *Code civil* defines "presumptions" as "Consequences drawn by the law or the magistrate from a known to an unknown fact."[2] Legal presumptions provide a way of filling in – at least pro tem – the gaps that obtain in conditions of incomplete information. (The "presumption of innocence" provides a paradigm example here.)

Such a legal presumption (*praesumptio juris*) is an inference from a fact that, by legal prescription, stands until refuted. Presumption of

---

[1] There is also a different – presently irrelevant – sense of the term in which it means "to lay claim to a merit or good without having done anything to deserve it." This is akin to the sort of self-aggrandizement or self-assertion at issue with *hubris*.

[2] "*Conséquences qui la loi ou le magistrat tire d'un fait connu à un fait inconnu.*" Bk. III, pt. iii, sect, iii, art. 1349.

this sort is a gap-filling resource: it comes into operation only in the absence of relevant information or evidence, and it leaves the scene once suitably strong evidential indications come to view. One authority has elucidated the conception of presumption in the following terms:

A presumption in the ordinary sense is an inference.... The subject of presumptions, so far as they are mere inferences or arguments, belongs, not to the law of evidence, or to law at all, but to rules of reasoning. But a legal presumption, or, as it is sometimes called, a presumption of law, as distinguished from a presumption of fact, is something more. It may be described, in [Sir James] Stephen's language, as "a rule of law that courts and judges shall draw a particular inference from a particular fact, or from particular evidence, unless and until the truth" (perhaps it would be better to say 'soundness') "of the inference is disproved."[3]

A legal presumption is thus a supposition relative to the given facts – a supposition that, by legal prescription, is to stand until refuted.

The tabulation of Display 1.1 lists some typical instances of legal presumption.[4] In every case the qualifying addendum "absent proof or evidence to the contrary" can and should uniformly be appended to the statement of such presumptive stipulations. The presumptions they specify can and should hold good until such time as counterindications come to view. For a presumption is not a fact but a provisional estimate of the facts. It is defeasible but nevertheless secure until actually defeated: it remains in place unless and until it is displaced by destabilizing developments.

Legal presumption specifies an inference that is to be drawn from certain facts in the absence of better information; it indicates a conclusion that, by legal prescription, is to stand until duly set aside, on the model of the "presumption of innocence." In many cases the legal presumption at issue can be defeated by appropriate evidence to the contrary. Presumption of this sort is sometimes called an argument *from* ignorance, but this is really not quite right; it is an argument *in* ignorance. For ignorance is not a ground or premise for which to reason but a circumstance in which one reasons as best one can, faute

---

[3] Sir Courtenay Ilbert, art. "Evidence," *Encyclopaedia Britannica*, 11th ed., Vol. 10 (Cambridge, 1910), pp. 11–21 (see p. 15).

[4] For one elaborate survey of legal presumptions, see Burr W. Jones, *The Law of Evidence, Civil and Criminal*, Vol. I, 5th ed. (San Francisco: Bancroft-Whitney, 1958).

- That a person accused of a crime is innocent
- That a child born in wedlock is legitimate, as is one born within eleven months of the husband's death
- That a person missing for seven years or more is dead
- That a regularly solemnized marriage is valid
- That a younger and healthier decedent survived longer in a common fatal accident of otherwise unknown result
- That agents are sane
- That people acting deliberately intend the actual consequences of their actions
- That young children (under the age of seven) cannot commit a felony
- That a child under fourteen has no criminal intent
- That an incriminating object found on the premises of a suspect is something that belongs to this individual
- That a person is cognizant of a contention clearly stated within his or her earshot
- That a document over 30 years old is genuine

DISPLAY 1.1. Some legal presumptions

de mieux to the resolution of an issue that needs to be settled. Sometimes, however, legal presumptions are indefeasible – for example, that a mature agent knows the law ("ignorance of the law is no excuse") or that in criminal matters one spouse is incompetent to testify against the other. The idea of presumptions is principally procedural in serving to determine what has to be done in the course of developing a cogent case.

It is clear that there are various sorts of rationales for presumptions. Some are a priori matters of procedural convenience or propriety (e.g., that someone is "innocent until proven guilty"); others are empirically guided by evidential backing (e.g., that someone missing for more than seven years is dead.) But, irrespective of their *grounding*, the operative functioning of presumptions is substantially the same. In every case, a presumption is a plausible pretender to truth whose credentials may well prove insufficient, a runner in a race it may not win. The "acceptance" of a proposition as a merely presumptive truth is not acceptance at all but a highly provisional and conditional epistemic inclination toward it, an inclination that falls far short of outright commitment.

Presumptions by nature provide a provisional surrogate for outright claims to the actual truth. As Lalande's philosophical dictionary puts it: "Presumption, speaking strictly and precisely, is an anticipation of something yet unproved."[5] A presumption is in tentative and provisional possession of the cognitive terrain, displaced by something that is evidentially better substantiated.[6] A presumption is a putative fact which, while in the circumstances perhaps no more than probable or plausible, is nevertheless to be accepted as true provisionally – allowed to stand until concrete evidential counterindications come to view. Presumption is thus typified by the idea of "innocent until proven guilty."

And so presumptions, though possessed of significant probative weight, will in general be defeasible – that is, subject to defeat in being overthrown by sufficiently weighty countervailing considerations. In its legal aspect, the matter has been expounded as follows:

[A] presumption of validity . . . retains its force in general even if subject to exceptions in particular cases. It may not by itself state all the relevant considerations, but it says enough that the party charged should be made to explain the allegation or avoid responsibility; the plaintiff has given a reason why the defendant should be held liable, and thereby invites the defendant to provide a reason why, in this case, the presumption should not be made absolute. The presumption lends structure to the argument, but it does not foreclose its further development.[7]

The standing of a presumption is thus usually tentative and provisional rather than absolute and final. A presumption stands only until the relevant issues that "remain to be seen" have been clarified, so that it

---

[5] André Lalande, *Vocabulaire de la philosophie*, 9th ed. (Paris: Presses Universitaires de France, 1962), s.v. "présomption": "*La présomption est proprement et d'une manière plus précise une anticipation sur ce qui n'est pas prouvé.*"

[6] The modern philosophical literature on presumption is not extensive. When I wrote *Dialectics* (Albany: State University of New York Press, 1977) there was little apart from Roland Hall's "Presuming," *Philosophical Quarterly*, 11 (1961): 10–22. More recently there is Edna Ullmann-Margalit, "On Presumption," *Journal of Philosophy*, 80 (1983): 143–63. A most useful recent overview is Douglas N. Walton, *Argumentation: Schemes for Presumptive Reasoning* (Mahwah, N.J.: Lawrence Erlbaum, 1996), which does, however, overlook our present central theme of probability. I am also grateful to Sigmund Bonk for sending me his unpublished study "Vom Vorurteil zum Vorausurteil."

[7] Richard A. Epstein, "Pleadings and Presumptions," *University of Chicago Law Review*, 40 (1973–4): 556–82.

becomes apparent whether the presumptive truth will in fact stand up once everything is said and done.[8]

The idea of potential defeasibility is critical for presumption. There are no indefeasible presumptions – whatever may seem to be such is in fact simply a stipulation or fiat. To be sure, certain legal principles are sometimes characterized as "conclusive presumptions" (for example, that a child of less than seven years cannot commit a crime or that a crime exists only with establishment of circumstances "beyond reasonable doubt"). But these indefeasible "presumptions" are presumptions in name only – in actual fact they are incontestable legal postulates. Strictly speaking, the idea of an "irrefutable presumption" is a contradiction in terms. Accordingly, such legal rules of ineligibility as

- that a wife is incompetent to testify against her husband

and

- that a minor is too immature to vote or to enter into a valid contract

are not presumptions but postulates or stipulations. Unlike presumptions, they are not defeasible but stand come what may. And while some legal theorists characterize such stipulations as conclusive (or irrebuttable) presumptions, this is unhelpful because it throws together items whose nature and function are altogether different.

---

[8] C. S. Peirce put the case for presumptions in a somewhat different way – as crucial to maintaining the line between sense and foolishness:

> There are minds to whom every prejudice, every presumption seems unfair. It is easy to say what minds these are. They are those who never have known what it is to draw a well-grounded induction, and who imagine that other people's knowledge is as nebulous as their own. That all science rolls upon presumption (not of a formal but of a real kind) is no argument with them, because they cannot imagine that there is anything solid in human knowledge. These are the people who waste their time and money upon perpetual motions and other such rubbish. (*Collected Papers*, VI, 6.423; compare II, 2.77 6–7.)

> Peirce is very emphatic regarding the role of presumptions in scientific argumentation and adduces various examples – for example, that the laws of nature operate in the unknown parts of space and time as well as in the known, or that the universe is inherently indifferent to human values and does not on its own workings manifest any inclination toward being benevolent, just, or wise. Peirce saw one key aspect of presumption to revolve about considerations regarding the *economics of inquiry* – that is, as instruments of efficiency in managing time and money. On this section of his thought, see N. Rescher, *Peirce's Philosophy of Science* (Notre Dame, Ind.: University of Notre Dame Press, 1978).

A presumption is not something that certain facts *give* us by way of substantiating evidentiation: it is something that we *take* through a lack of counterevidence. A presumption is more akin to a theft than a gift. It is not authorized by what we know about a particular matter; it is something eminently useful to which we help ourselves because we can get away with it. In the legal context, Wigmore puts the matter as follows:

> If they [the jury] find the fact of absence for seven years unheard from, and find no explanatory facts to account for it, then *by a rule of law they are to take for true the fact of death,* and are to reckon upon in accordingly in making up their verdict upon the whole issue.[9]

As this indicates, the matter of *taking for granted* is pivotal for presumption.

Accordingly, presumption is certainly not knowledge: we do not *know* what we merely *presume* to be so. As an informative resource its standing is quite different from that of knowledge acquired by learning. But it nevertheless is an informative resource – and a highly useful one at that, since it serves to close up an otherwise debilitating gap.

On this basis, the idea of presumption is also closely linked to that of a default position in information science. Suppose you are confronted with a variety of alternatives $A_1, A_2, \ldots A_n$. And you take the stance that alternative A_1 is to be adopted in the absence of a clear-cut demonstration that some other alternative is appropriate. Then this is standardly designated as the *default position* for this choice of alternatives. And this is effectively tantamount to presuming the appropriateness of A_1, retaining it in place unless and until a specific reason for change comes to view.

Presumptions will vary in point of their probative weight. Some legal presumptions stand until overturned by a conclusive refutation even as the presumption of innocence in criminal matters requires refutation "beyond a reasonable doubt." Still others merely impose a burden of persuasion that reflects a balance of probability (e.g., that the parties to an agreement are sane). And so there are weaker and stronger presumptions.

---

9 John Henry Wigmore, *The Principles of Judicial Proof: A Treatise on the Anglo-American System of Evidence in Trials at Common Law,* Vol. 10 (Boston: Little, Brown, 1904–1905; 3rd ed. 1940), sect. 2490. Issues relating to presumption and burden of proof are extensively canvassed in this classic work on legal reasoning.

The conception of a prima facie case is intimately connected with that of burden of proof. To make out a prima facie case for one's contention is to adduce considerations whose evidential weight is such that in the absence of countervailing considerations, the "reasonable presumption" is now in its favor, and the burden of proof (in the manner of an adequate reply that "goes forward with [counter] evidence") is now incumbent on the opposing party. What is at issue with cognitive presumption is a social process of dialectical interaction, a practice in information management that provides for socially sanctioned entitlements whose appropriateness is substantiated by the efficacy of established practice in matters of communal inquiry and communication.

Their inherent defeasibility means that appropriate presumptions are impervious to occasional failure. However, what is defeasible about a presumption is not the general rule (e.g., that people missing for seven years are dead) but its application in a particular case (that Smith who has been missing for seven years is indeed dead). Presumptions thus stand secure against occasioned failures in point of successful application. They are safeguarded by that explicitly protective clause: unless and until there are indications to the contrary.

2. Presumptions as Procedural Resources

Presumptions are inherently in *procedural* injunctions. This is illustrated by the presumption of innocence-in-the-absence-of-proven-guilt which is, in effect, a conditional inferential mandate taking the following form:

Whenever the (antecedent) premises *P* obtains one is authorized to infer the conclusion *C* in the absence of explicit indications to the contrary.

Legal presumptions are generally mandates based on rules that do not merely authorize but require. B. W. Jones puts the matter as follows:

A presumption may be defined to be an inference *required* by a rule of law drawn as to the existence of one fact from the existence of some other established basic facts – It is a true presumption of fact in the sense that another fact is assumed from established basic facts. It is a presumption of law in the sense that a rule of law requires the assumption to be made.[10]

Elsewhere, however, rules of presumption are often mere inference licenses. The practice at issue, be it mandatory or an authorization, will differ in its nature from context to context, operating within the limits of appropriate practice of the domain of praxis that is in question (law, communication, rational inquiry, or whatever). Honoring these presumptions is in each case a matter of "the rules of the game" that define the project at issue.

Presumptive reasoning in general has a very definitive structure along the following lines:

- A presumptive principle of generic import
- A particular case subsumed under this principle
- A specific, particularized presumption
- A determination of nonexceptability
- A specific conclusion

This general pattern is illustrated by the following inference:

- There is a standing presumption that a person missing for seven years is dead.
- John Smith has been missing for seven years.
- John Smith may be presumed dead.
- There is no reason to see this presumption as defeated (say, by evidence of deception or fraud).
- John Smith is dead.

Here of course the status of the conclusion is not that of an established fact but rather just exactly that of a valid presumption.

As the preceding illustrations indicate, presumptive reasoning represents a process that moves from a generic presumption of general principle via a specific (principle-instantiating) situation to a factual conclusion of presumptive standing. And so without general principles of presumption there can be no presumptive claims whatsoever and specific presumptions must necessarily be "covered" by such generic rules.

---

[10] Burr W. Jones, *The Law of Evidence, Civil and Criminal*, Vol. I, 5th ed. (San Francisco: Bancroft-Whitney, 1958).

A rule of presumption contrasts with a corresponding universal generalization. Compare (a) the presumption that a person missing for seven years is dead, and (b) the factual generalization "People missing for seven years are always dead." Note that this presumption is valid (legally appropriate) even though the universal generalization is incorrect. Universality is dispensable for presumption, nor does presumptive appropriateness even require statistical generality. Thus contrast (a) the presumption that the accused is innocent of a crime until proven guilty of it with (b) the proposition that people accused of a crime are usually innocent of it unless their guilt can be proven in a court of law. It may well be – indeed presumably is – actually the case that most of the time the people accused of a crime did actually commit it. Nevertheless that presumption remains a perfectly appropriate legal principle. Presumptions are validated by their functional efficacy within their operative context and not by their statistical accuracy.

Legal presumption exists to foster the functions of law or the interests of social management. As instrumentalities effective in facilitating public ends they need not directly reflect matters of empirical fact. The presumption of innocence does not rest on the fact that accused individuals are generally innocent. Nor does the presumption that a person absent for seven years dies immediately upon the expiration of this period reflect the determinable facts of the matter.[11] Presumptions have a life of their own determined correlative with the objectives in whose service they are operative.

3. Presumption beyond the Law

From its role in the courtroom, presumption migrated into the area of disputation, which served as an important process in the teaching method of medieval universities. It was pivotal for the theory of academic disputation via the obligations (*obligationes*) seen as incumbent upon a disputant to support his assertions by appropriate argument

---

[11] These considerations cast a large shadow of doubt over the U.S. Superior Court's contention that a presumption is "an inference as to the existence of a fact not actually known arising from its *usual connection* with another which is known" (Jones, The Law of Evidence, p. 16). For adequacy in the case of presumptions of law, that italicized phrase should be changed to *legally mandated connection*.

- That a newly introduced contention requires substantiation.
- That the substantiation provided is the best and most plausible that there is.
- That an uncontested contention is conceded as true.
- That a proposition attested by established authorities is true.
- That in a context of contentions the stronger arguments prevail.

DISPLAY 1.2. Dialectical presumptions

(*agenti incumbit probatio*).[12] On this basis we encounter such presumption as are listed in Display 1.2. And thus employment of the mechanisms of presumption in disputation finds an ongoing resonance in its role in the exercise of debating that continues popular in schools and colleges to the present day.[13]

Of special importance here is the governing idea that the supporting argument provided in a disputation must strive for maximum plausibility. In consequence, the presumption is that the grounds a disputant adduces in support of his or her contentions represent, as this disputant sees it, the strongest arguments there are.

With disputation and dialectics serving as an intermediary, the use of presumption then moved on to find application in a wide variety of further cognitive contexts including the theory of communication, of rational inquiry, and of the methodology of scientific investigation. It is, in fact, one of epistemology's most fruitful conceptions for there is, in most probative contexts, a standing presumption in favor of the usual, normal, customary course of things. And so with presumption we *take* to be so what we could not otherwise manage to *establish*. And presumptions set the stage for many of our interpersonal actions and activities. In general we presume that one's interagents are pursuing in good faith the aims and objectives of whatever project we are

---

[12] See Eleonore Stump and P. V. Spade, "Obligations," in Norman Kretzmann (ed.), *The Cambridge History of Later Medieval Philosophy* (Cambridge: Cambridge University Press, 1998), pp. 315–41. And on the logical underpinnings of medieval disputation see Hajo Keffer, *De Obligationibus: Rekonstruction einer spätmittelalterlichen Disputationstheorie* (Leiden: Brill, 2001). Keffer rightly stresses the connections that link medieval disputation with the dialectics discussed in Aristotle's *Topics*.

[13] See for example Gerald H. Sanders, *Introduction to Contemporary Academic Debate*, 2nd ed. (Prospect Heights, Ill.: Waveland Press, 1983); F. H. Van Eeinemen, *Fundamentals of Argumentation Theory* (Mahwah, N.J.: Lawrence Erlbaum, 1996).

interactively engaged in with them – be it a game, a discussion, an inquiry, or a collaborate or competitive venture of any sort.

Law and rhetoric apart, presumptions figure importantly in many other areas of cognitive endeavor. After all, the idea is virtually ubiquitous of "making a good case" for what one maintains, so it is only natural and to be expected that a legal resource such as presumption would find applications elsewhere. Most prominently this includes

- *communication* (To presume that people mean what they say)
- *inquiry* (To presume the correctness of the most strongly evidentiated answer to a question for which an answer is required)
- *science* (To presume the simplest of equally eligible explanations is correct)
- *philosophy* (To presume that philosophical problems are tractable)

The ensuing pages will examine in closer detail how presumptions function in these various domains.

However, not everything that looks to be a plausible presumption actually is one. Thus Louis Katzer considers it a "presumption of justice" that people whose condition is the same in point of issue-relevant respects should be treated alike – that is, that people should receive the same treatment unless and until grounds for dissimilarity of treatment have been established.[14] But what is actually at issue here is less a presumption of justice than a broader principle of rational procedure, namely the "Principle of Sufficient Reason." In general, when there is (by hypothesis) no reason whatever for treating two cases differently, it is clear that rational people will not do so.

Some writers see presumption as merely an action-guiding device.[15] But this does not do full justice to the matter. For while a practice is indeed at issue with presumption, this can also include the practice of information management – of epistemic or cognitive procedure.

With presumption's origins firmly fixed in the realm of law, there are two alternative directions in which the topic can be developed. It

---

[14] See Louis I. Katzner, "Presumptions of Reason and Presumptions of Justice," *Journal of Philosophy*, 70 (1973): 89–100.

[15] "Presumption rules belong to the realm of praxis, not theory. Their point is to enable us to get on smoothly with business of all sorts . . . to facilitate and expedite action" (Edna Ullman-Margalit, "On Presumption," *Journal of Philosophy*, 80 (1983): 143–63; see p. 147.

can be pursued in the direction of the rhetoric of public discourse in the area of social and political affairs, or in the theory of knowledge in matters of inquiry and communication. It is the latter alternative that will be at issue in this book.[16]

---

[16] The former alternative is at issue in an excellent and erudite book by Richard H. Gaskins, *Burdens of Proof in Modern Discourse* (New Haven: Yale University Press, 1992). Writing about my earlier work in *Dialectics* (Albany: SUNY Press, 1977), Gaskins observes (p. 281) that its treatment of the dialectic of burden of proof "does not, however, associate its logical functions with cultural, social, and organizational elements." This will be true of the present book as well.

2

Presumption and Burden of Proof

1. Introduction

Presumption is closely bound to the idea of burden of proof (*onus probandi*), which is also at root a legal conception. It functions in the context of an adversarial proceeding in which one party is endeavoring to establish and another to rebut some charge before a neutral adjudicative tribunal. The very phrase (*onus probandi*) derives from classical Roman law where it affords one of the ground rules of probative procedure, governing the division of the labor of argumentation between plaintiff and defendant, which specifies tasks of marshaling evidence. Under the Roman system, nothing was conceded in legal actions as admitted: the plaintiff, as the initiating agent in laying a charge, had to make his case first (*agenti incumbit probatio*), then the defendant's countercase was argued on his *exceptio*, and thereafter the plaintiff's on his *replication*, and so on. The burden rested with the plaintiff in civil cases and with the state (as surrogate plaintiff) in criminal cases. Throughout, the "burden of proof" lay with the side active in making the allegations, subject to the fundamental rule that "the need for proof lies with him who affirms, not him who denies."[1]

The idea of burden of proof embodies a basic ground rule of the probative process. To say that the burden of proof rests with a certain

---

[1] *Necessitas probandi incumbit ei qui dicit non ei qui negat.* See Sir Courtenay Peregrrine Ilbert, art. "Evidence," *Encyclopedia Brintannica*, 11th ed., Vol. 10, pp. 11–21 (see p. 15).

side is to say that side must adduce the substantiation required to make its case. Thus with the presumption of innocence, the prosecution is, in criminal law, obliged to present to the court at least a prima facie case for maintaining the guilt of the accused. This is to be accomplished by furnishing information sufficient to show the guilt of the accused in the absence of counterevidence. In California, for example, a level of blood alcohol in excess of 1/10 percent (as indicated by a blood or breath test administered to a driver at the scene of an arrest) is considered prima facie evidence of driving while intoxicated. But of course the development of such an initial case can be rebutted by the deployment of further evidence (e.g., by the defense showing that the inebriated person was merely a passenger in the vehicle, not its driver).[2] A presumption indicates that in the absence of specific counterindications we are to accept in the present case how things are "as a rule," and it places the burden of proof upon the adversary's side to show that this acceptance would not be appropriate.

Various aspects of Anglo-American legal procedure revolve around this rule of presumption in allocating the burden of proof. And the "Scots verdict" of *Not proven* affords a way of saying that the burden has been discharged in part, sufficiently for the correlative presumption (of innocence) to come to an end, without, however, an actual proof of guilt having been fully established.[3] In everyday-life situations we generally presume that the truth lies on the side of a strong argument that constitutes a powerfully indicative case, even if it relies on some circumstantial evidence. This stance does not, however, carry over to criminal law.

Burden of proof and presumption represent correlative conceptions, inseparably coordinated with one another throughout the range of rational inquiry. They are, in effect, opposite sides of the same coin, either as throwing the advantage of a presumption on one side, or as throwing the burden of proof on the other. For with any defeasible presumption there is the issue of what is necessary to effect such a defeat. And in any epistemic situation in which the idea of burden

---

[2] For an informative exposition of the legal issues, see Richard A. Epstein, "Pleadings and Presumptions," *University of Chicago Law Review*, 40 (1973/4): 556–82.

[3] These issues and many others that bear upon the concerns of this chapter are treated in that classic work on legal reasoning, John Henry Wigmore, *The Principles of Judicial Proof* (Boston: Little, Brown, 1913; with numerous later editions).

of proof can figure, the very "rules of the game" remain inadequately defined until a suitable determination has been made regarding the nature, extent, and weight of the range of presumptions that are to be operative. In effect, a presumption is coordinate with – or to be more exact, is simply the reverse of – a burden of proof (of the "burden of further reply" variety). The existence of a presumption places upon anyone who would deny its application in a particular case the burden of producing good reasons for doing so in the circumstances at hand.

2. Burden of Proof and of Reply

Presumption – and the idea of burden of proof that is indissolubly connected to it – also serves as a fundamentally dialectical conception and has figured as such from classical antiquity to Hegel and beyond.[4] As a dialectical resource, presumption points towards two rather different sorts of things. One authority has put the matter as follows:

In modern law the phrase "burden of proof" may mean one of two things, which are often confused – the burden of establishing the proposition at issue on which the case depends, and the burden of producing evidence on any particular point either at the beginning or at a later stage of the case. The burden in the former sense ordinarily rests on the plaintiff or prosecutor. The burden in the latter sense, that of going forward with evidence on a particular point, may shift from side to side as the case proceeds. The general rule is that he who alleges a fact must prove it, whether the allegation is construed in affirmative or negative terms.[5]

Accordingly there are really two distinct, albeit related, conceptions at issue with regard to "burden of proof":

(1) The *probative burden of an original assertion*: the initiating burden of proof. The basic rule is: "Whichever side initiates the assertion of a thesis within the dialectical situation has the burden of supporting it in argument." The champion of a thesis – like the champion of a medieval joust – must be prepared to maintain his side in the face of the opposing challenges. This burden of *agenti incumbit probatio* remains constant throughout.

---

[4] On this aspect of the matter, see Rescher, *Dialectics* (Albany: State University of New York Press, 1977).

[5] Ilbert, "Evidence," p. 15.

Whether we are dealing with legal or with cognitive matters, it is only reasonable that someone who wants to upset that status quo and go against the established and accustomed course of things should bear the burden of producing good reasons for so doing.

But there is also another aspect to the matter.

(2) The *dialectical burden of further reply in the face of contrary considerations*. Whenever considerations of significant evidential bearing have been adduced, this argument may be taken as standing provisionally until some sufficient reply has been made against it in turn. Thus the opponent of any contention – be it an assertion or a denial – always has the "burden of further reply." This "burden of going forward with evidence (or counterevidence)," as it is sometimes called, may shift from side to side as the dialectic of controversy proceeds.

The former mode, initiating burden, is static and rests with the inaugurating side constantly and throughout; the latter, dialectical burden, involves the idea that a suitably weighty amount of evidence can manage to *shift* the burden from one side to the other as the course of argumentation proceeds. This second type of burden is crucial. It embodies the imperative of "advancing the argument" in a meaningful way, carrying the discussion forward beyond a particular stage of its development. And in doing so, it implements one of the key functions of the process of controversy.

A key presumption of rational dialectic is that the truth is more likely to lie on the side of a really powerful argument. And so whenever appropriately weighty counterarguments are adduced for a contention, the burden of persuasion shifts to the other side. In this regard, presumption reverses like a shuttlecock in both rational deliberation and in the rhetorical dialectics of thesis and objection, denial and reaffirmation. The key idea here is that of adducing probative considerations whose force is "sufficient" to reverse the burden of proof, shifting the weight of argument from one side to the other:

The effect of a presumption is to impute to certain facts or groups of facts a *prima facie* significance or operation, and thus, in legal proceedings, to throw upon the party against whom it works the duty of bringing forward evidence to meet it. Accordingly, the subject of presumption is intimately connected with the subject of burden of proof, and the same legal rule may be expressed in different forms, either as throwing the advantage of a presumption on one side, or as throwing the burden of proof on the other.[6]

In line with this idea, the circumstance that the burden of proof always rests upon the party initially asserting a thesis lends to the view that there is automatically a *presumption against* any maintained thesis. But, of course, if the adducing of evidence in the dialectic of rational argumentation is to be possible at all, this circumstance must have its limits. Clearly, if the burden of proof inclined against *every* contention, if there were an automatic presumption of falsity against any contention whatsoever, it would become in principle impossible ever to constitute a persuasive case. The rule that every substantive contention needs evidential support through the adducing of further substantiating contentions cannot reasonably be applied ad indefinitum.

3. The Weight of a Burden

This idea of probative sufficiency leads immediately to the *weight* of the burden of proof or of the *strength* of presumption, to look at it from another angle. British law, for example, adopts different standards of proof in criminal and civil cases. In criminal cases guilt must be established "beyond reasonable doubt"; in civil cases it is sufficient to show that the defendant is guilty "on the balance of probabilities." And both standards are flexible. In criminal cases, "What is reasonable doubt... [should vary] in practice according to... the punishment which may be awarded."[7] Moreover, "the standard of proof for cases of fraud is the civil one of preponderance of probabilities, but what is 'probable' depends upon the heinousness of what is alleged... 'in proportion as the offense is grave, so ought the proof to be clear.'"[8] Generally, in law (and in disputation as well), what will be evidentially sufficient in shifting a burden of proof hinges on the inherent seriousness of the contention at issue. For mere evidentiation is in general inconclusive and on this basis will usually not establish outright truth

---

[6] Epstein, "Pleadings," pp. 556–82.

[7] Epstein. "Pleadings," pp. 558–60.

[8] Sidney L. Phipson, *The Law of Evidence* (London: Stevens and Haynes, 1892; 11th ed., 1970), p. 230.

but only provide for an increasingly strong presumption. It is only presumption – but not necessarily demonstration – that lies on the side of the strongest aspects in rational deliberation.

In effect, a defeasible presumption is just the reverse of a burden of proof (of the "burden of further reply" variety). Whenever there is a "burden of proof" for establishing that p is so, the correlative defeasible presumption is that not-p stands until the burden has been discharged definitively. In his classic work on rhetoric, Archbishop Whately formulated the relationship at issue in the following terms:

According to the most current use of the term, a "presumption" in favour of any supposition means, not (as has been sometimes erroneously imagined) a preponderance of probability in its favour, but such a *preoccupation* of the ground as implies that it must stand good till some sufficient reason is adduced against it; in short, that the *burden of proof* lies on the side of him who would dispute it.[9]

It is in just this sense, for example, that the "presumption of innocence" in favor of the accused is correlative with the burden of proof carried by the state in establishing his guilt.

A presumption, whatever it be, is going to remain in place – safe and secure for the time being – until the burden of proof incumbent on anyone seeking to invalidate it has been effectively discharged. Thus presumptions will differ in strength according to just how much it takes to defeat them – that is, on just how great a burden of proof is being carried by anyone seeking to defeat them. Presumptions are *strong* or *weak* as their associated burden is *heavy* or *light*. Thus in Anglo-American law the presumption of legitimacy and of innocence are strong and require effectively conclusive evidence for their rebuttal, whereas the presumption of sanity is weak.[10]

---

[9] Richard Whately, *Elements of Rhetoric* (London and Oxford: John Murry and J. F. Parker, 1827), Pt. 1, Ch. III, Sect. 2. A reprint edited by Douglas Ehninger was issued in Carbondale by the University of Illinois Press in 1963. For a modern discussion of Whately's position see J. Michael Sproule, "The Psychological Burden of Proof: On the Evolutionary Development of Richard Whately's Theory of Presumption," *Communicative Monographs*, 43 (1976): 115–29. Whateley's classic discussion of the subject is still one of the most instructive treatments of presumption.

[10] On this issue see *Durham v. United States*, 241f 2d 862 (D. C. Circuit 1954), pp. 741–49.

4. Cognitive Rationality and Burden of Proof

It cannot be emphasized too strongly that the idea of burden of proof is not a strictly *logical* concept, considered in the realm of rational *inference*. Logic in itself has no dealings with the issue of probative obligations or even with the (categorical) truth status or presumptive truth status of propositions. After all, logic's concern with truth is not substantive and categorical but proceeds wholly in the hypothetical mode ("If certain theses are [assumed to be] true, then certain others must also be [assumed to be] true"). And so, rather than being a logical concept, burden of proof is a *methodological* one. It has to do not with valid or invalid reasoning, but with probative argumentation in dialectical situations. The workings of the conception of burden of proof represent a *procedural or regulative principle of rationality* in the conduct of argumentation: a ground rule, as it were, of the process of rational controversy – a fundamental condition of the whole enterprise.

While the rule that every contention requires evidential support through the adducing of further substantiating contentions cannot reasonably be made regressively operative ad indefinitum, this does not mean that there must be *unquestionable* theses, theses that are inherently uncontestable, totally assured, and irrefutable.

To take this view in matters of cognition would involve a misreading of the probative situation. It is to succumb to the tempting epistemological doctrine of foundationalism, that insists on the need for and ultimate primacy of absolutely certain, indefeasible, crystalline truths, totally beyond any possibility of invalidation. And this sort of thing is entirely dispensable. However, when "accepting" a thesis as presumptively true, one concedes it a probative status that is strictly provisional and pro tem; there is no need here to invoke the idea of *unquestionable* theses, theses that are inherently uncontestable, certain, and irrefutable.[11]

---

[11] On the strictly empirical side, it is difficult to exaggerate the extent to which our processes of thought, communication, and argumentation in everyday life are subject to established presumptions and accepted plausibilities. This is an area that is only beginning to be subjected to sociological exploration. (See, for example, Harold Garfinkel, *Studies in Ethnomethodology* [Englewood Cliffs, N.J.: Prentice Hall, 1967].) The pioneer work in the field is that of Alfred Schutz, *Der sinnhafte Aufbau der sozialen Welt* (Wien: J. Springer, 1932).

The search for such self-evident or protocol theses – inherently inviolate and yet informatively committal about the nature of the world – represents one of the great quixotic quests of modern philosophy.[12] The philosophers' theory of knowledge here puts usage with the ways in which we deal with the matter in everyday life. For the epistemic quest for categories of data that are prima facie acceptable (such as innocent until proven guilty) is altogether different from this quest for absolutely certain or totally self-evidencing theses that has characterized the mainstream of epistemological tradition from Descartes via Brentano to Roderick Chisholm.

But there really is no need for this sort of thing. The probative requirements of disputational dialectic do not involve any category of irrefutable claims. All we need is that some theses, or rather, some types of theses are such that the presumption of truth inclines in their favor – that the burden of proof is to be carried by someone who wishes to reject a contention of this sort. Once a thesis of this type is introduced and substantiated, however imperfectly, there is a pro tem presumption of truth in its favor, one that persists until it is overthrown in its turn. The crucial thing, then, is the availability of certain families of contentions that inherently merit the "benefit of doubt," that are able to stand provisionally – that is, until somehow undermined; in short, however vulnerable to refutation, they have a presumption of acceptability in their favor. There is, in this domain, a crucial contrast between "decisive" (or "conclusive") evidence and "prima facie" evidence – the former resulting from the latter only if it is not defeated or overridden by further countervailing considerations.[13] Such inconclusive evidence yields presumptions which, though possessed of significant probative weight, will in general be defeasible – that is, they are subject to defeat in being overthrown by sufficiently weighty countervailing considerations. In its legal aspect, the matter is expounded by one writer as follows:

---

[12] This is not the place to address the skeptic's insistence on the certainty of knowledge in a manner so hyperbolic that it is unavailable in practice. The relevant issues are canvassed in Rescher, *Scepticism* (Oxford: Blackwell, 1980).

[13] Although *probability* can in certain circumstances serve as a guide to presumptions, complications do arise in this connection. We cannot pursue the issue here, but refer the reader to the discussion in Rescher, *Plausible Reasoning* (Assen: Van Gorcum, 1976). On the legal aspects of the presumptive role of probabilities, see Epstein, "Pleadings," pp. 580–82.

[Such] a presumption of validity . . . retains its force in general even if subject to exceptions in particular cases. It may not by itself state all of the relevant considerations, but it says enough that the party charged should be made to explain or deny the allegation to avoid responsibility; the plaintiff has given a reason why the defendant should be held liable, and thereby invites the defendant to provide a reason why, in this case, the presumption should not be made absolute. The presumption lends structure to the argument, but it does not foreclose its further development.[14]

Where the burden of proof is allocated – and when necessary reallocated – the concept of presumption plays a pivotal epistemological role in the structure of rational argumentation. Clearly there must be some class of claims that are allowed at least pro tem to enter uncontested into the framework of argumentation, because if everything were contested, the process of inquiry could not progress at all. Such a class may, but need not, constitute a stable category. It could be determined on a contextual basis, by strictly *local* (rather than *global*) ground rules – so that theses that figure as presumptions in some situations need not do so in others. Above all, presumptions are not uncontestable. In "accepting" a thesis as such, one concedes it a probative status that is strictly provisional and pro tem; one does *not* say to it: "Others abide our question, thou art free."

A "reasonable assumption" is in general one that is well evidentiated: if it looks like a duck, and quacks like a duck, and waddles like a duck, the reasonable assumption is that it *is* a duck. A presumption, on the other hand, is rendered reasonable by conforming to a well-established *practice* (or general rule) of taking something to be so. It is not a matter of evidence or substantiation but of authorization through an established probative practice. (To be sure, a good many reasonable assumptions have little to do with presumption as such. If you are handling an unknown gun it is sensible to do so with care under the reasonable supposition that it might be loaded. But there is no presumption at work here. In most circumstances, at any rate, it is not a general rule that guns are loaded.)

How does presumption differ from presupposition? Presupposition is a logico-conceptual relationship between statements: one claim or contention presupposes another if it makes no sense when this other

---

[14] Epstein, "Pleadings," pp. 558–59.

fails to obtain. (That someone *lost* a race presupposes that this individual actually competed in it and not simply that he is one among the myriad people who did not win it.) Presumption, by contrast, belongs not to language as such but to the modus operandi of language users. It belongs to the order of pragmatics – of linguistic praxis like lying or deceiving. Presuming is part of the modus operandi not of language but of language uses. Like "to know" or "to believe" or "to conjecture," "to presume" is a cognitive verb that relates people with facts or probative facts. It does not relate such facts with one another, but characterizes the nature of the relationship between an inquirer and a putative fact.

A contention becomes a presumption through our making it so by presuming it. Of course the fact at issue (e.g., someone's being dead when long lost) is true or false (whatever it be) independently of ourselves. But the status of being a presumption is (like the status of being an assumption or a belief or a regret) the product of something we do in relation to this (purported) fact. In a world without minds there can be a multitude of facts but no assumptions or hypotheses or presuppositions – or, for that matter, presumptions.

The rational legitimation of a presumptively justified belief lies in the fact that some generic mode of "suitably favorable indication" speaks on its behalf while no already justified counterindication speaks against it. When, after a careful look, I am under the impression that there is a cat on the mat, I can (quite appropriately) base my acceptance of the contention "There is a cat on the mat" not on certain preestablished premises, but simply on my experience – on my visual impression. The salient consideration is that there just is no good reason (in *this* case) that one should not indulge one's inclinations to endorse a visually grounded belief of this kind as veridical. (If there were such evidence – if, for example, I was aware of being in a wax museum or a magician's studio – then the situation would, of course, be altered.)

The presumptive justification of beliefs – unlike their discursive justification – need not proceed through the evidential meditation of previously justified grounds but directly and immediately through the force of a "presumption." A belief is justified in this way when there is a *standing presumption* in its favor and no circumstantially case-specific reason that stands in the way of its acceptance. Such beliefs of this sort are appropriate – are rationally justified – as long as nothing speaks against them. In this case, presumption is the epistemic analogue of "innocent until proven guilty."

5. Presumption and Skepticism

Of course, various objections might be offered against the very idea of defeasible presumptions: "How can you speak of maintaining or accepting a proposition merely as a presumption but not as a truth? If one is to assert (accept, maintain) the proposition in any way at all, does one not thereby assert (accept, maintain) *it to be true?*" The answer here is simply a head-on denial, for there are different modes of acceptance. To maintain P as a presumption, as *potentially* or *presumptively* factual, is akin to maintaining P as possible or probable or plausible. In no case are these contentions tantamount to maintaining the proposition as flat-out true. Putting a proposition forward as "possible" or "probable" commits one to claiming no more than that it is "possibly true" or "probably true." Similarly, to assert P as a presumption is to say no more than that P is potentially or presumptively true, that it is a promising truth-candidate – but does not say that P is actually true, that it is a truth. Acceptance does not lie along a one-dimensional spectrum that ranges from "uncertainty" to "certainty." There are not only degrees of acceptance but also kinds of acceptance. And presumption represents such a kind: it is sui generis, and not just an attenuated version of "acceptance as certain."

In fact, however, the conception of a presumption does not "open the floodgates" in an indiscriminate way. Not *everything* qualifies as a presumption: the concept is to have some probative bite. A presumption is not merely something that is "possibly true" or that is "true for all I know about the matter." To class a proposition as a presumption is to take a definite and committal position with respect to it, so as to say "I propose to accept it as true insofar as no difficulties arise from doing so."

There is thus a crucial difference between an alleged truth and a presumptive truth. For allegation is a merely rhetorical rather than epistemic category: every contention that is advanced in discussion is "allegedly true" – that is, alleged-to-be-true. But presumption – that is, warranted presumption – is an *epistemic* category: only in certain special circumstances are contentions of a systemic *sort* that they merit being accepted as true provisionally, "until further notice."[15]

The idea of presumptive truth must thus play a pivotal role in all such various contexts in which the notion of a "burden of proof" applies. The mechanism of presumption accomplishes a crucial epistemological task in the structure of rational argumentation. There must clearly be some class of claims that are allowed to be at least provisionally accepted within the framework of argumentation, because if everything were contested, the process of inquiry could not progress at all.

If rationally justified belief must always be based upon rationally prejustified inputs, then a vitiating situation would arise and skepticism would become unavoidable. If this were the case, the process of rationally validating our accepted beliefs could never get started. To all appearances, we here enter upon a regress that is either vitiatingly infinite or viciously circular. The rational justification of belief becomes in principle impossible – as skeptics have always insisted.

But this particular skeptical foray rests on a false footing, for the rational justification of a belief does *not* necessarily require prejustified inputs. The important distinction between *discursive* and *presumptive* justification becomes crucial here in a way that skeptics conveniently overlook.

A belief is justified *discursively* when there is some other preestablished belief on whose basis this belief is evidentially grounded, that is, when the belief is substantiated by some particular item of supporting evidence. The discursive justification of a belief lies in there being an already available, prejustified belief that evidentiates it. In information-processing terms, this discursive sort of justification is not innovative but merely transformatory as a production process: there must be justified beliefs as inputs to arrive at justified beliefs as outputs. (We would be in sad straits were it so – for then the process of justification would recede into the darkness of an infinite regress.) However, *discursive* justification is not the only sort there is; there is also *presumptive* justification.

---

[15] For further details regarding the important role of presumptions in the philosophical theory of knowledge, see Rescher, *Methodological Pragmatism* (Oxford: Basil Blackwell, 1976).

In any essentially dialectical situation in which the ideas of presumption and burden of proof figure, the very "rules of the game" remain inadequately defined until the issue of the nature, extent, and weight of the range of operative presumptions has been resolved in some suitable way. Burden of proof and presumption represent correlative conceptions inevitably coordinate with one another throughout the context of rational dialectic, because the recourse to presumptions affords the indispensable means by which a burden of proof can – at least provisionally – be discharged.

Presumptively justified beliefs are quite sufficient to provide the raw materials for processes of rational deliberation. They represent contentions that – in the absence of preestablished counterindications – are acceptable to us "until further notice," thus permitting us to make a start in the venture of cognitive justification without the benefit of prejustified materials. They are defeasible, vulnerable to being overturned, but only by something else yet more secure, some other preestablished conflicting consideration. They are entitled to remain in place until displaced by something superior. Accordingly, their impetus averts the dire consequences that would ensue if any and every cogent process of rational deliberation required inputs that themselves had to be authenticated by a *prior* process of rational deliberation – in which case the whole business could never get under way.

The reality is that we cannot pursue the cognitive project – the quest for information about the world – without undertaking certain initial presumptions. They are reminiscent of Kantian "conditions under which alone" – requisites in whose absence the business of securing answers to questions about the world could not make a successful start. In matters of sense perception, for example, we presume that mere appearances ("the data") provide an indication of how things actually stand (however imperfect this indication may ultimately prove to be). That we can use the products of our experience of the world to form at least somewhat reliable views of it is an indispensable presupposition of our cognitive endeavors in the realm of factual inquiry. If we systematically refuse, always and everywhere, to accept *seeming* evidence as *real* evidence – at least provisionally, until it is discredited as such – then we can get nothing by way of informative cognition. A skeptic sufficiently extreme to reject any and all presumptions would thereby automatically block any prospect of reasoning with him within the standard framework of inquiry regarding the empirical facts of the world. The process of presumptions is part and parcel of the mechanisms that define probative rationality, and abandoning it would abort the entire project at the very outset.

Burden of proof carries an impetus to stability and conservation. However, it does not have this impetus because of some underlying idea that the status quo is invariably or generally optimal and superior to its alternatives. Rather, it has this impetus on the basis of rather different considerations. To begin with, there are always various alternatives: given that we are where we are, there is always a plurality of different directions in which to move. And to move on we have to do so in one or another of these directions: we cannot get on our horse and ride off in all of them at once. And until a particular direction is decided on as superior to the rest (staying put included) there is neither point nor motivation for moving on. To justify shifting from the status quo we need a cogent rationale for identifying a particular alternative as superior to the status quo. It is this circumstance – rather than some sort of presumptive superiority – that endows the status quo with its advantage in point of burden-of-proof considerations. The matter is once again one of rational economy of process. There is no point in expanding the effort needed to effect a change for the status quo until this step receives some warrant from the angle of cost-benefit considerations. Various recent writers have been distrustful of the seemingly conservative aura that has enveloped burden-of-proof considerations since the days of Bishop Whateley's *Elements of Rhetoric* (1827).[16] But this disinclination fails to acknowledge that what is fundamentally at issue is a matter not of ideological conservatism but of mere practical rationality.

[16] See Chaim Perelman and L. Olbrechts-Tyteca, *The New Rhetoric: A Treatment on Argumentation* (Notre Dame, Ind.: University of Notre Dame Press, 1969), p. 103; and also Richard H. Gaskins, *Burdens of Proof in Modern Discourse* (New Haven: Yale University Press, 1992), p. 24.

3

Cognitive Presumption and Truth

1. Cognitive Fundamentals

Presumptions obtain principally with two ends in view. On the one hand there are the purely *cognitive* presumptions made for the sake of answering our questions and filling gaps in our information (as, for example, presumptions regarding the reliability of sources). On the other hand there are *practical* presumptions made for the sake of guiding our decisions regarding actions (as with legal presumptions that facilitate the resolution of cases; for example, that someone long missing is dead so that the person's estate can be distributed). At present, however, the cognitive sector of presumption will be at the focus of concern, with presumption as a source of (putative) information about the truth of things in the forefront.

A cognitive presumption stakes a claim that outruns the substance of actually available information; it is a proposition that, in suitably favorable circumstances, is accepted as true in the absence of any counterindications. This is a default position affording an answer to some question of ours that we adopt for lack of anything better and will keep in place until such time as something comes along to eject it from this position of favor. In this way, cognitive presumptions function as instrumentalities of rational economy. Thanks to them we need not remain bereft of answers to our questions until all the relevant returns are in – which is to say virtually never.

The deliverances of our own experiences – the "testimony of our senses," for example – generally provide for presumptions of just this sort. To be sure, in the late twentieth century a whole generation of epistemologists turned against the idea of "the experientially given." They insisted that in this context *experientially given* means "given as a categorical truth," thence inferring the consequence that the unattainability of factual certainty means there are no experiential givens at all. But of course the situation is drastically transformed when one acknowledges that beyond the given *as true*, there is also the given *as plausible or presumptive*. Once this step is taken, the issue of "the epistemic bearing of sensory experience upon our knowledge" acquires a very different aspect. Thus consider the salient question: Does the fact that I take myself to be seeing a cat on a mat – that I have a "seeing a cat on a mat" experience – "entitle" or "authorize" me to adopt the belief that there actually is a cat on the mat over there? This question, once raised, leads back to the underlying questions: What is at issue with belief *entitlement* in such a context? Does it require guaranteed correctness beyond the reach of any prospect of error – however far-fetched and remote? Clearly the answer is Surely not! Presumptions, after all, are not certified truths. A presumption represents a claim to truth that, however plausible, may in the end not be able to make good, seeing that presumptions are defeasible, and may in the end have to be abandoned. We are fair-weather friends to our presumptions: when things get bad enough we will unashamedly abandon them. Entitlement and justification for a presumptive claim is no more than the sort of rational assurance that it makes sense to ask for in the context at issue: a matter of reasonable suggestion rather than categorical proof. The fundamental question, after all, need not and should not be "Does subjective experience *unfailingly guarantee* its objective proportions?" but rather "Does it *appropriately indicate* it?" And it is in the light of this distinction between establishing and presumptifying (to coin a useful if awkward neologism) that the idea of "the experientially given" must be construed.

The principal theses of these deliberations regarding the epistemic bearing of sensory experience upon our knowledge can thus be set out at follows:

1. There indeed are experiential givens. But these "givens" are actually "takens." They are not products of inference (hence

"givens") but of an epistemic endorsement policy or practice (hence "takens").

2. Most critically, those experiential givens are not "givens as categorically and infallibly true" but rather as merely plausible. What is at issue is not something *categorically certified* but merely something *presumptive*.

3. The move from plausibility to rationally warranted acceptance ("justified belief") is automatic in those cases where *nihil obstat* – that is, whenever there are no case-specific counterindications.

4. Although this way of proceeding does not deliver categorical guarantees or infallible certitude, such things are just not required for the rational validation (or "epistemic justification") of belief.

5. On this basis, subjective experience can – and does – validate our claims to objective factual knowledge. But the step at issue in moving across the subjectivity/objectivity divide is indeed a step – a mode of praxis. And the modus operandi at issue in this practice or policy is at once validated by experience and established through a complex process in which rational and natural selection come into concurrent operation.[1]

The important epistemic role of presumptions in the cognitive domain makes it desirable to take a closer look at what is at issue here.

Presumption is not the same as assumption – let alone presupposition. To be sure, in presuming something we assume (or suppose) it to be so: a presumption is an assumption (or supposition). But the reverse is not the case: not any old assumption (or supposition) is a presumption. We can assume something to be so for the sake of discussion or argument or deliberation. But here the result is a mere hypothesis while a presumption is something we actually accept.

The prime difference between mere hypotheses and presumptions lies in the distinction between IF and SINCE. One's stance toward

---

[1] The epistemological program this essay sketches out combines ideas set out in considerable detail in several of my publications: *The Coherence Theory of Truth* (Oxford: Oxford University Press, 1973), *Plausible Reasoning* (Assen: Van Gorcum, 1976), *Methodological Pragmatism* (Oxford: Basil Blackwell, 1977), *Scepticism* (Oxford: Blackwell, 1980), *Human Knowledge in Idealist Perspective* (Princeton: Princeton University Press, 1991), *A Useful Inheritance* (Pittsburgh: University of Pittsburgh Press, 1994).

hypotheses is noncommittal and experimental: we undertake hypotheses to see what happens if. But our stance toward presumptions is committal – even if only provisionally. We accept them until such time (if ever) when impeding obstacles arise.

This point was already stressed by Leibniz long ago, when he wrote:

> What is called *presumption* is incomparably more than a mere *supposition*, for suppositions should generally be admitted only when proved, whereas anything that is spoken for by a presumption must be allowed to pass for true until refuted.... [Presumption] has the force of transferring the *onus probandi* to the opposite side, thus saddling it with the burden of proof.[2]

To say all this is not, of course, to say that the plausibilistic route to accommodating the probative bearing of sensory experience and other informative resources is the only possible approach to accounting for this sort of evidence. But it is, clearly, one efficient and effective way to rationalize credibility in such matters and provides a straightforward and efficient way to proceed.

In any situation of rational deliberation or discussion, the fundamental burden of proof always inclines against the agent who presents a thesis for acceptance, but one must, of course, make it *possible* for him to build a substantiating case. The marshaling of supporting considerations must be something that is not made infeasible in principle: not *everything* can be disqualified from the very outset as failing to count as available in this regard. All rational discussion and deliberation presupposes an exchange of considerations, and it will not do in such a context simply to abort the entire process at the start by denying probative cogency to any and every contention whatsoever.

Accordingly, it must be acknowledged that there are always *some* considerations that are "allowed to count" toward providing an at least provisional substantiation. And so there must always be established ground rules acknowledging certain categories of contentions as endowed with evidential weight. It makes sense to speak of a "burden of proof" only in the context of established rules regarding the discharge of such a burden. In rational controversy, there must always be some impartially fixed common ground determining what is to

---

[2] Leibniz to M. Jacquelot, 20 November 1702. In C. I. Gerhard (ed.), *Die philosophischen Schriften von G. W. Leibniz*, Vol. 3 (Berlin: Weidmann, 1887), p. 444.

count as evidence for acceptance as true. And it is just here that the principle of presumption comes into its own.

The reason for *the* prominence of presumption in matters of cognition is straightforward. As beings who must act to live and who guide their creators by their beliefs, we members of homo sapiens have questions and need answers. But in this life we have few categorical guarantees. Where are the truths of seventeenth-century science, and where will those of our science be in the year 3000? If the business of presumption did not already have a place in our cognitive arsenal it would have to be invented. And indeed it was!

2. Some Aspects of Cognitive Presumption

A tradition in philosophical epistemology that reaches from the later Stoics and Academic Skeptics of antiquity to the British Idealists of the turn of the present century insists (not always *expressis verbis*, but in effect) on a presumption of truth in favor of the deliverances of memory and of the senses. Theses based on observation or recollection are to have the benefit of doubt, a presumption of truth in their favor – they are to stand unless significant counterindications are forthcoming. Moreover, we standardly operate with a good many other epistemic presumptions, some of the most important of them being listed in Display 3.1

- To believe the evidence of your own senses
- To accept at face value the declarations of other people
- To accept the determinacy of such standard "sources" of information as the senses and memory
- To accept the declarations of recognized experts and authorities within the area of their expertise
- To trust in the reliability of the standardly employed cognitive aids and instruments (telescopes, calculating machines, reference works, logarithmic tables, etc.)
- To accept those answers to your questions for which the available evidence speaks most strongly

DISPLAY 3.1. Some rules of cognitive presumption. *Note*: Throughout there is the qualifying proviso: *In the absence of specific indications to the contrary.*

Consider just one example. Against the claims of the senses or of memory automatically to afford us the truth pure and simple, one can deploy all of the traditional arguments of the skeptics. And, in particular, we have before us the admonition of Descartes: "All that up to the present time I have accepted as most true and certain I have learned either from the senses or through the senses; but it is sometimes proved to me that these senses are deceptive, and it is wiser not to trust entirely to any thing by which we have once been deceived."[3] But, of course, any such skeptical dismissal of the potential of sensory data serves only to reemphasize their role as presumptions – provisionally acceptable truth-claims in our presumptive sense rather than outright *truths* as such.[4] They represent contentions that merit being accepted as true provisionally, "until further notice," until the path to acceptance is clear, in that the crucial issue that "remains to be seen" has been clarified – that is, whether the presumptive truth will in fact stand up once "everything is said and done."

A further key instance of cognitive presumption is afforded by sources that we can reasonably take to be reliable and which, for that very reason, yield information that we can also reasonably accept. This occurs with particular prominence in the context of expertise and authoritativeness. In recognizing people as experts or authorities in a certain field we presume that these individuals "know what they are talking about." This presumption in turn leads us to suppose that when such individuals state a claim within the field of their expertise, it may reasonably be assumed to be true. The presumption that underwrites the credibility of expert and authoritative sources is a prime instance of this phenomenon. And this holds not only for "experts" and people we can expect to be "in the know" but also for such impersonal sources of information as instruments or inferential processes. Thus one can not only presume that the information afforded by an encyclopedia is correct (having presumably been written by experts) but proceed likewise with "authorities" at large.

To be sure, throughout these epistemic contexts a developmental process is at work that pivots on the prospect of changing what was

---

[3] René Descartes, *Meditations on First Philosophy*, No. I (tr. by R. M. Eaton).

[4] The defeat of a defeasible presumption relates (in the case of a specific presumption of fact) to its upset by falsification in a particular instance rather than the distinction of the presumption rule as such. Of course, such a general rule or principle – the presumptive veracity of a reliable source, for example – can also be *invalidated* ("falsified" would he inappropriate). (For a further discussion of the relevant issues, see Rescher *Methodological Pragmatism* [Oxford: Basil Blackwell, 1976].)

initially a mere presumption to something validated by experience. Thus, for example, it is the statistical record that will ultimately teach us about the reliability of experts. Cognitive presumption is thus part of ongoing information development – of learning – and is not a matter of dogmatic closure.

3. Principles of Presumption

Presumptions can be either concrete and specific or abstract and generic. That long-lost individuals are dead is a generic presumption, that Smith who has been missing for many years is dead is a specific presumption – the former in a general rule, the latter a specific application thereof. However, generic presumptions are fundamental. Any acceptable specific presumption must be based on an appropriate generic presumption as an instance thereof. Thus I presume that Dr. X is a qualified medical practitioner because he was listed as such in the yellow pages of the telephone directory. And I presume that his diagnosis of my ailment is correct because I accept him (via the previous presumption) to be a qualified physician. Presumptions, like Shakespearean troubles, come not as single spies but in battalions, with specific presumptions invariably grounded in generic principles.[5]

Any appropriate cognitive presumption either is or instantiates a general rule of procedure of the form that to maintain P whenever the condition C obtains unless and until the standard default proviso D (to the effect that countervailing evidence is at hand) obtains. [Thus: to maintain an individual's innocence whenever this person is accused of a crime unless and until this person's guilt is duly established.] From the standpoint of the logic of the situation this rule takes the form of

$$C \Rightarrow (\sim D \Rightarrow P)$$

or more elaborately with explicit provision for specific cases,

$$(\forall x)(C(x) \Rightarrow [\sim D(x) \Rightarrow P(x)]).$$

---

5 Consideration of the rule of presumption in logic and the theory of knowledge goes back to Richard Whately, *Elements of Rhetoric* (London and Oxford: Oxford University Press, 1928). The theme was reintroduced into the contemporary scene in Rescher, *Dialectics* (Albany: SUNY Press, 1972). See also E. Ullman-Margalit, "On Presumption," *Journal of Philosophy*, 80 (1983): 143–63, and Douglas N. Walton, *Argumentation Scheme for Presumptive Reasoning* (Mahwah, N.J.: Lawrence Erlbaum, 1996).

A rule of cognitive presumption accordingly has three parts: a condition (C), a default proviso (D), and a presumptive conclusion (P). Whenever a particular conclusion is maintained via the operation of such a principle – that is, whenever $P(a)$ is assessed in a specific case a on the basis that $C(a)$ and $\sim D(a)$ – then the resultant proposition $P(a)$ is itself characterized as being of the status of a presumption (rather than an established fact). And the crucial fact of the matter is that the only way to realize a particular presumption is through the application of a suitable principle of presumption.

That boiler-plate default proviso P is crucial with presumptions owing to their inevitable defeasibility. However, it is quite clear that such loose attachment to a presumption is by no means tantamount to no attachment at all.[6] For a presumption stands secure only "until further notice," and it is perfectly possible that such notice might be forthcoming.

For a proposition to count as a presumption is altogether different from its counting as a truth, just as a man's being a presidential candidate is something far different from his being a president. Plausible truth-candidacy does not require or presuppose truth: quite different issues are involved. The "acceptance" of a proposition as a presumptive truth is not *acceptance* at all, but a highly provisional and conditional epistemic inclination toward it, an inclination that falls far short of outright commitment.

What stops a presumption from being a mere assumption or hypothesis is the aspect of compulsion – be it juridically or rationally mandated – inherent in the fact that a presumptive principle normatively makes a normative stipulation regarding *what is to be done*. Assumptions after all are free options – one can make them or not as one is minded. A presumption by contrast is grounded in the compelling authority of the law in the one case and of the demands of reason on the other.

---

[6] I. Scheffler puts a similar point in the temporal context of changing one's mind in the light of new information: "That a sentence may be given up at a later time does not mean that its present claim upon us may be blithely disregarded. The idea that once a statement is acknowledged as theoretically revisable, it can carry no cognitive weight at all, is no more plausible than the suggestion that a man loses his vote as soon as it is seen that the rules make it possible for him to be outvoted" (*Science and Subjectivity* [Indianapolis, Ind.: Bobbs-Merrill, 1967], p. 118).

4. Defeasibility and the Role of Presumption

Consider the contention, "If you take away one grain from a heap of sand you will still have a heap." This altogether plausible thesis cannot be maintained dogmatically as holding always and invariably, lest one encounter the Heap Paradox (Sorites) that has intrigued logic theorists since classical antiquity. The thesis holds in general and by and large, but not invariably. In the normal, general run of cases we can proceed on its basis, but occasional problems are bound to arise. The thesis is not a flat-out truth but should be seen as affording a presumption on whose basis we can in general proceed without undue concern. What is offered is not a secure fact – a flat-out truth – but merely a reasonable presumption.

Though we accept our cognitive presumptions we do so only provisionally. Thus recognizing that our cognitive presumptions are defeasible and hold good only "until further notice," we confront the question of what can defeat a presumption. Principally, three things:

1. *Stronger presumptions to the contrary.* The unanimous contrary testimony of more witnesses, for example, or the contrary opinion of a more experienced and knowledgeable expert.
2. *Counterevidence.* We presume that the individual who has "gone missing" for many years is dead, but if he reappears "big as life," that's that.
3. *Inconsistency.* When reference work *A* tells me something I presume it as correct. But when the equally authoritative reference work *B* tells me something else that conflicts, that previous presumption is canceled out.

An element of *putativity* or *presumption* will thus always be present with any inquiry procedure whose findings are inherently defeasible. As long as defeasibility prevails, there can be no absolute and inevitable rational *constraint* to acceptance. The procedure does not – *ex hypothesi* – yield certified and irrevocable truths, so a suspension of judgment always remains a viable alternative in the face of defeasibility. The most such a defeasible rational inquiry procedure can accomplish is to determine what one *should* accept *if* one is minded to accept anything at all in the circumstances of the case. Its incapacity to produce unconditionally and unqualifiedly certified truths means that its products are to be regarded in the light of *putative* or merely *presumptive* truths. (A claim to truth may, of course, be reasonably advanced in circumstances in which an altogether definitive rational guarantee of truth may yet not be forthcoming.)

5. Presumptive Truth

And so, a presumption is not so much a "given" as a "taken." But a proposition may be *taken* in two ways:

1. Taken *for good as a truth or as actually true*, to be definitively classed as true, and
2. taken *on approval* as a *truth-candidate* or as *potentially or presumptively true*; to be classed as true provisionally – that is, provided that doing so creates no problems or anomalies.

Now a presumption is a proposition that is "taken" not in the first, unqualified mode, but only in the second: it is a surrogate truth – a *claimant* or *pretender* to truth whose credentials may well prove insufficient, a runner in a race it may not win.

The unqualified *acceptance* of a thesis is, to be sure, a decisive act. But the prospect of provisional acceptance means that one can take tentative and indecisive steps in its direction. Initially accepted with hesitation on some slight provisional and probatively insufficient basis, a thesis can build up increasing trust. A fundamentally economic analogy holds good here: a thesis, like a person, can acquire a solid credit rating only by being *given* credit (i.e., *some* credit) in the first place – provisionally and without any very solid basis.

Accordingly a cognitive presumption is no more than a putative truth, accepted tentatively as a proposition that one is to class as true *if one can*, that is, if doing so generates no difficulties or inconsistencies. The starting of a presumption is provisioned: it is not *established* as true; it is backed only by a rationally warranted expectation that it may turn out true "if all goes well." It is a prima facie truth in exactly the sense in which one speaks of prima facie duties in ethics. A prima facie "duty" amounts to an actual duty provided only that no countervailing conditions are operative. Similarly, a presumption is a prima facie "truth" in that the evidentiations are sufficiently positive that under the circumstances we are prepared to class it as *actually true* provided that no countervailing considerations are operative. It lays a claim to truth, but it may not be able to make good this claim in the end. But a claim to truth – even one that is advanced hesitatingly and provisionally – is still just that: a claim to truth. *It is altogether wrong to equate a tentative claim to truth with a claim to tentative truth!* They are every bit as different as a hesitant confession of wrongdoing and a confession of hesitant wrongdoing. Because a claim to truth is provisional does not render it a claim to provisional truth.

This distinction between certified truths and merely presumptive truth-candidates demands emphasis because it is central to present purposes. Any *experiential* justification of a truth-criterion must pull itself up by its own bootstraps – it needs factual inputs, but yet these factual inputs cannot at this stage already qualify as truths. To meet this need it is natural to appeal to truth-candidates, data that are no more certified *truths* than candidate-presidents are certified presidents – though some of them are ultimately bound to win out.

In this context, plausibility connects with the idea of evidentiation or substantiation. As ample experience shows, it is emphatically not the case that in answering our questions in situations of incomplete information it is always the best-evidentiated alternative that turns out to be true. But it is, nevertheless, an altogether reasonable policy to adopt the practice of proceeding on this presumption via the following rule:

> The best and most strongly evidentiated answer to a question is to be presumed correct.

Evidence does not ensure truth; it does no more than provide a presumptive induction of it. Its function is not that of a guarantee but that of a presumption.

There is, of course, no blinking at the fact that "*p* is *presumptively* true" does not *mean* "*p* is true." With presumption as with assertion there remains the "gap of commitment" between the thesis itself and the stance that some subscribers take toward it. Defeasibility relates to the epistemic status of truth-claims, not to their nature as being perfectly authentic claims *to truth*. The concept of truth continues to be prominently operative, and this is not abrogated when truth-claims are put forward in a way recognized as ultimately tinged with some touch of provisionality. There is thus no need whatever to take the view that a fallibilistic approach casts the idea of truth in a merely regulative role as governing only the ultimate aims of inquiry without any relevance to the here-and-now.[7]

All the same, we do not intend the conception of a cognitive presumption to "open the floodgates" in an indiscriminate way. Not everything is a presumption: the concept is to have some logico-epistemic bite. A presumption is not merely something that is "possibly true" or that is "true for all I know about the matter." To class a proposition as a presumption is provisionally to take a definite and committal position with respect to it. However, this provisional endorsement is still a matter of endorsement as true. Defeasibility relates to the epistemic status of truth-claims, not to their nature as being perfectly authentic claims *to truth*. The concept of truth continues prominently operative: it is not abrogated by taking the view that truth-claims are put forward in a way recognized as ultimately tinged with some touch of provisionality.[8]

Presumptive truths generally do not stand alone. They inhere in rules or principles and of practice thereby come in clusters or families in coordination with the relevantly operative principle of presumption. The ancient theorists of knowledge usually construed these groupings in terms of the epistemic *sources* from which the theses at issue have their provenance. The "data of memory" and the "deliverances of the senses" were the paradigmatic cases then envisaged. Such an approach seems perfectly reasonable – presumptions should be understood as forthcoming systematically and pervasively in terms of some general policy, method, or procedure.

---

[7] C. S. Peirce sometimes inclined in the direction of this view, and K. R. Popper accepted it outright. See his *Objective Knowledge* (Oxford: Clarendon Press, 1972), pp. 19–30.

[8] This section and the next one draw on my paper "The Illegitimacy of Cartesian Doubt," first published in *The Review of Metaphysics*, 13 (1959): 226–34 and reprinted with some revisions in *Essays in Philosophical Analysis* (Pittsburgh: University of Pittsburgh Press, 1969). For an interesting treatment of cognate issues see Robert Almeder, "Fallibilism and the Ultimate Irreversible Opinion," in N. Rescher (ed.), *Essays in the Theory of Knowledge* (Oxford: Basil Blackwell, 1975; *American Philosophical Quarterly* Monograph, no. 9), pp. 33–54.

6. Presumption and Plausibility

On medieval views linking plausibility and presumptions see Hajo Keffer, *De Obligations* (London: Brill, 2001), pp. 181–86.

One important device for putting the idea of cognitive presumption to work is the conception of plausibility as determined by circumstantial evidentiation and probative substantiation in general.[9] In effect we have the following principle of presumption:

> Whenever a certain supposition is not only plausible but also more plausible than its potential rivals, it may be presumed to be true.

For plausibility can serve as the crucial determinant of where presumption resides. The basic principle here is this rule:

> Presumption favors the most *plausible* of rival alternatives – when indeed there is one. This alternative will always stand until set aside (by the entry of another, yet more plausible, presumption).

The operation of this rule creates a key role for plausibility in the theory of reasoning and argumentation.[10] In the face of discordant considerations, one "plays safe" in one's cognitive involvements by endeavoring to maximize the plausibility achievable in the circumstances. Such an epistemic policy is closely analogous to the *prudential* principle of action – that of opting for the available alternative from which the least possible harm can result. Plausibility-tropism may be seen as an instrument of epistemic prudence. Plausibility accordingly emerges as a pivotal mechanism of rational (as opposed to conventional) dialectic.

The standing of sources in point of their comparative authoritativeness is also a critical factor seeing that a thesis is more or less plausible depending on the reliability of the sources that vouch for it – their entitlement to qualify as well informed or otherwise in a position to stake claims to credibility. It is on this basis that "expert testimony"

---

[9] Historically this goes back to the conception of "the reasonable" (*to eulogon*, as discussed in Greek antiquity by the Academic Skeptics). Carneades (c. 213-c. 128 B.C.) for one worked out a rather well-developed (nonprobabilistic) theory of plausibility as it relates to the deliverances of the senses, the testimony of witnesses, and so on. For a helpful discussion of the relevant issues, see Charlotte L. Stough, *Greek Skepticism* (Berkeley and Los Angeles: University of California Press, 1969).

[10] On these issues see Rescher, *Plausible Reasoning* (Assen: Van Gorcum, 1976).

and "general agreement" (the consensus of men) come to count as conditions for plausibility.

Of course the probative strength of confirming evidence also serves as a substantive basis of plausibility. On this basis, the rival thesis whose supporting case of substantiating evidence is the strongest is thereby the most plausible. Our evidential resource will thus play a key role in regard to plausibility.

The plausibility of contentions may, however, be based not on a thesis-warranting *source or evidentiation* but a thesis-warranting *principle*. Here inductive considerations may come prominently into play; in particular, such warranting principles are the standard inductive desiderata: simplicity, uniformity, specificity, definiteness, determinativeness, "naturalness," and so on. In such an approach one would say that the more simple, the more uniform, the more specific a thesis – either internally, of itself, or externally, in relation to some stipulated basis – the more emphatically this thesis is to count as plausible.

For example, the concept of *simplicity* affords a crucial entry point for plausibility considerations. The injunction "Other things being anything like equal, give precedence to simpler hypotheses vis-à-vis more complex ones" can reasonably be espoused as a procedural, regulative principle of presumption – rather than a metaphysical claim as to "the simplicity of nature." On such an approach, we espouse not the Scholastic adage "Simplicity is the sign of truth" (*simplex sigilium veri*), but its cousin, "Simplicity is the sign of plausibility" (*simplex sigilium plausibili*). In adopting this policy we shift the discussion from the plane of the constitutive/descriptive/ontological to that of the regulative/methodological/prescriptive.

Again, uniformity can also serve as a plausibilistic guide to reasoning. Thus consider the *Uniformity Principle*:

In the absence of explicit counterindications, a thesis about unscrutinized cases which conforms to a patterned uniformity obtaining among the data at our disposal with respect to scrutinized cases – a uniformity that is in fact present throughout these data – is more plausible than any of its regularity-discordant contraries. Moreover, the more extensive this pattern-conformity, the more highly plausible the thesis.

This principle is tantamount to the stance that when the initially given evidence exhibits a marked logical pattern, then pattern-concordant claims relative to this evidence are – ceteris paribus – to be evaluated as more plausible than pattern-discordant ones (and the more comprehensively pattern-accordant, the more highly plausible). This rule implements the guiding idea of the familiar practice of judging the plausibility of theories and theses on the basis of a "sufficiently close analogy" with otherwise validated cases.[11] (The uniformity principle thus forges a special role for the prioritization of *normality* – of "the usual course of things" – in plausibility assessment.)[12]

In general, the more plausible a thesis, the more smoothly it is consistent and consonant with the rest of our knowledge of the matters at issue. Ordinarily, the removal of a highly plausible thesis from the framework of cognitive commitments would cause a virtual earthquake; removal of a highly implausible one would cause scarcely a tremor. In between we have to deal with varying degrees of readjustment and realignment. And in general, the closer its fit and the smoother its consonance with our cognitive commitments, the more highly plausible the thesis. Systemic interconnectedness and plausibility thus go hand in hand in a way that renders presumption as a key factor in inductive reasoning.[13]

---

[11] All this, of course, does not deal with the question of the status of this rule itself and of the nature of its own justification. It is important in the present context to stress the *regulative* role of plausibilistic considerations. This now becomes a matter of *epistemic policy* ("Give priority to contentions which treat like cases alike") and not a metaphysically laden contention regarding the ontology of nature (as with the – blatantly false – descriptive claim "Nature is uniform"). The plausibilistic theory of inductive reasoning sees uniformity as a *regulative principle of epistemic policy* in grounding our choices, not as a *constitutive principle* of ontology. As a "regulative principle of epistemic policy" its status is *methodological* – and thus its justification is in the final analysis pragmatic. See Rescher, *Methodological Pragmatism* (Oxford: Basil Blackwell, 1976).

[12] See Ferdinand Gonseth, "La notion du normal." *Dialectica*, 3 (1947): 243–52, as well as Rescher, *Philosophical Standardism* (Pittsburgh: University of Pittsburgh Press, 1994).

[13] For a closer study of the notion of plausibility and its function in rational deliberation, see Rescher, *Plausible Reasoning* (Assen: Van Gorcum, 1976) and *Induction* (Oxford: Basil Blackwell, 1980). On the principles of plausible reasoning in the natural sciences, see Norwood R. Hanson, *Patterns of Discovery* (Cambridge: Cambridge University Press, 1958), and his influential 1961 paper "Is There a Logic of Discovery?" in H. Feigl and G. Maxwell (eds.), *Current Issues in the Philosophy of Science*, Vol. I (New York: The Free Press, 1961). The work of Herbert A. Simon is an important development in this area: "Thinking by Computers" and "Scientific Discovery and the Psychology of Problem Solving" in R. G. Colodny (ed.), *Mind and Cosmos* (Pittsburgh: University of Pittsburgh Press, 1966).

7. Presumption and Probability

When I have a "seeing the cat on the mat" experience – that is, when I have an experience on the basis of which I find myself accepting that "there is a cat on the mat over there," then "I am under the impression that I am looking at a cat on yonder mat." Does this experience and its resulting impression and inclination "justify" me in claiming "There is a cat on the mat"? Yes and no. In and of itself no. But in the setting and against the background of a wider and larger course of experience on whose basis I have learned that these virtually based belief inclinations are by and large true – unlike dream experiences or "hunches" of various sorts – it transpires that I am indeed "justified." That justification does not, however, lie in the visual experience alone but also within the entire functional context of learning that such visual experiences are by-and-large veridical. (Here again think of "the given" versus "the taken".)

Presumption is often seen as a matter of plausible conjecture, with probability taken. The pivotal principle here authorizes the presumption of the probable. On this basis we find in Rudolf Eisler's useful philosophical handbook the explanation "Präsumption (*praesumptio*): Voraussetzung aus Wahrscheinlichkeits-Gründen," representing presumption as a (pre)supposition that rests on considerations of probability.[14] Such an approach is not, however, free from difficulty.

Presumption aligns with plausibility, but the plausibility of a thesis will not necessarily be a measure of its *probability* – of how likely we deem it, or how surprised we would be to find it falsified. Rather, it reflects the prospects of its being fitted into our cognitive scheme of things in view of the standing of the sources or principles that vouch for its inclusion herein. The core of plausibility is the notion of the extent of our cognitive inclination toward a proposition – of *the extent of its epistemic hold upon us* in the light of the credentials represented by the bases of its credibility. The key issue is how readily the thesis in view could make its peace within the overall framework of our cognitive commitments.

---

[14] Rudolf Eisler, *Handwörterbuch der Philosophie*, 2nd. ed. (Berlin: E. S. Mittler & Sohn, 1922), s.v. "Präsumption."

One of the cardinal lessons of modern epistemology is that considerations of probability cannot provide a validating basis for a flat-out claim to truth. This lesson is driven home by the so-called Lottery Paradox.

Thus suppose the threshold level to be 0.80, and consider the following series of six statements:

This (fair and normal) die will not come up *i* when tossed (where *i* is to be taken as 1, 2, 3, 4, 5, and 6, each in turn).

According to the specified standard, every one of these six statements must be accepted as true. Yet their conjunction results in the patent absurdity that there will be no result whatsoever. Moreover, the fact that the threshold was set as low as 0.80 instead of 0.90 or 0.9999 is wholly immaterial. And to reconstitute the same problem with respect to a higher threshold we need simply assume a lottery with enough (equal) divisions to exhaust the spectrum of possibilities with individual alternatives of sufficiently small probability. Then the probability that each specific result will *not* obtain is less then 1 minus the threshold value, and so can be brought as close to 1 as we please. Accordingly, we would, by accepting each of these claims and conjoining them into a single whole, be led straightaway into contradiction once more.

This, then, is the Lottery Paradox.[15] It decisively rules out a propositional acceptance standard that is based simply on a probabilistic threshold.[16]

Two important lessons with respect to presumption emerge in the light of these considerations: (1) The presumption that can appropriately be made on probabilistic ground depends on just exactly what the question context happens to be. And (2) since the plausibilities of different contexts may be incompatible, one cannot plausibly conjoin such presumptions across the board – detaching them from their question context and throwing them together. Plausible

---

[15] The Lottery Paradox was originally formulated by H. E. Kyburg, Jr., *Probability and the Logic of Rational Relief* (Middletown, Conn.: Wesleyan University Press, 1961). For an analysis of its wider implications for inductive logic see R. Hilpinen, *Rules of Acceptances and Inductive Logic* (Amsterdam: North-Holland Publishing Company, 1968; *Acta Philosophica Fennica*, fasc. 22), pp. 39–49. See also I. Levi, *Gambling with Truth* (New York: Knopf, 1967), chaps. 2 and 6.

[16] Cf. the discussion of this theme in Rescher, *Plausible Reasoning*.

presumption, that is to say, is an essentially "erotetic" process that provides a question-resolving resource. And whereas true answers are question-detachedly exportable across different problem contexts, plausible presumptions are not. In reasoning from merely plausible presumptions we must take special care to maintain the overall coherence and consonance of the claims to which we stand committed. Since presumptions are defeasible we will always have to keep a weather view to considerations that might defeat them.[17]

---

[17] Chapter 6, "Default Reasoning," will return to this issue.

4

Validating Cognitive Presumptions

1. The Purposiveness of Presumption

Whenever we act and actually do something on the basis of a *presumption* we take a step beyond it: we make the *assumption* that it is correct. This assumption may turn out to be incorrect. But even if so, this nevertheless does nothing to unravel the validity of that initial presumption in the circumstances under which it arose. Its erroneousness is a matter of hindsight unavailable before the fact and represents a misfortune rather than a mistake.

The appropriateness of presumptions is not to be assessed on an individualized retail basis; instead the matter is one of wholesale – of the statistically systemic appraisal of the principles of presumption that underlie the particular case. Presumption is a methodological and procedural resource and must be judged on that basis through its performance "on the whole." Thus epistemic presumptions exist to enhance our access to usable information, and communicative presumptions exist to facilitate the transmission thereof. The ultimate test of the appropriateness and validity of our presumptive proceedings in their various domains will be a matter of their efficacy in the realization of the correlative purposes – an ultimately pragmatic standard.

In the late nineteenth century, C. S. Peirce in the United States and Ernest Mach in Europe suggested an evolutionary rationale for certain presumptions such as trust in the senses and in various analogies.

Such features, so they maintained, have emerged in nature under the premises of evolutionary development, and if they were not effective, if they did not have at least a modest statistical tendency in the direction of veracity they would not have survived through the generations. There is considerable merit to this intriguing idea.

Let us consider the epistemic situation of a cat-on-the-mat experience, in which "I take myself to be seeing a cat on the mat." On this basis, I would arrive quite unproblematically at the following contentions:

- It seems plausible to suppose that there is a cat on the mat.
- There is presumably a cat on the mat.

But, of course, to claim unqualified assurance that there indeed is a cat on the mat would be stretching matters too far in the circumstances. Still, the indicated pro-inclination toward the thesis at issue is certainly warranted. To step from that subjective visual experience to an objective factual claim on the order of these,

- There actually is a cat there.
- There actually is a mat there.
- The cat is actually emplaced on the mat.

is one that presumes a great deal. Yet on what basis is such a presumption justified?

The step from a sensory experience ("I take myself to be seeing a cat") to an objective factual claim ("There is a cat over there and I am looking at it") is procedurally direct but epistemically mediated. And it is mediated not by an *inference* but by a *policy* – namely, the policy of trusting one's own senses, by a policy of presumption. And this policy itself is based neither on wishful thinking nor on arbitrary decisions: it emerges in the school of praxis from the consideration that a long course of experience has taught us that our senses generally guide us aright – that the indications of visual experience, unlike, say, those of dream experience, generally provide reliable information that can be implemented in practice.[1]

---

[1] But why does knowledge root in presumptions rather than probabilities (to take yet another mode of tentative cognition into view)? Ultimately, because there is no way of

Just what sorts of claims are presumptively justified? For one thing, ordinary and standard probative practice of empirical inquiry stipulates a presumption in favor of such cognitive "sources" of information as the senses and memory – or for that matter trustworthy personal or documentary resources such as experts and encyclopedias. And the literature of the subject further contemplates such cognitively useful alternatives as these:

> *Natural inclination* or a "natural disposition" to accept (e.g., in the case of sense observation)
> *Epistemic utility* in terms of the sorts of things that would, if accepted, explain things that need explanation
> *Analogy* with what has proved acceptable in other contexts
> *Fit* or coherence with other accepted theses

Thus even a weak reed like analogy – the assimilation of a present, problematic case to similar past ones – is rendered a useful and appropriate instrumentality of presumption through providing our readiest source of answers to questions.[2] However, the salient feature of a viable basis for principles of epistemic presumption is that they must have a good track record for providing useful information.

As the prior discussion has already stressed, our cognitive proceedings incorporate a host of epistemic presumptions of reliability. Throughout all such cases epistemic presumption favors the ordinary, the usual, and the natural – its tendency is one of convenience and ease of operation in cognitive affairs. And the crux here is that presumption is a matter of cognitive economy – of the eminently rational policy of following "the path of least resistance" to an acceptable conclusion. Its leading principle is to introduce complications only when

---

substantiating what is likely to be without a good deal of reference to what is actually the case, as per following line of reasoning:

- Whenever there are dark clouds on the horizon, rain is likely to come.
- There are dark clouds on the horizon.
- It will likely rain soon.

Probabilities, unlike presumptions, cannot be adequately grounded in policies; they must be grounded in purported facts.

[2] This is why adherence to custom is a cardinal principle of cognitive as well as practical rationality. Cf. William James, "The Sentiment of Rationality," in *The Will to Believe and Other Essays in Popular Philosophy* (New York: Longmans, Green, 1897).

you need to, always making do with the least complex resolution of an issue.

And so, the justification of presumption is, in the final analysis, purposive – a matter of future efficacy within the context of purpose in which the particular presumption at issue figures.

2. Justifying Presumptions

The justifactory rationale for a policy of epistemic presumption begins with the human need for information. And the obvious and evident advantage of presumption as a cognitive resource is that it enables us vastly to extend the range of questions we are able to answer. It affords an instrument that enables us to extract a maximum of information in situations of inquiry and communication. Presumption, in sum, is an ultimately pragmatic resource. It is a thought instrumentality that makes it possible for us to do the best we can in circumstances when something must be done. And so presumption affords yet another instance when practical principles play a leading role on the stage of our cognitive and communicative practice.

A cognitive presumption as such is not a thesis or theory: it represents a practical policy – a modus operandi. It seems helpful in this regard to draw a distinction between two sorts of procedural guides, namely, rules and principles. A rule is an instruction for how to proceed in concrete situations of various sorts. It addresses the choice among alternative courses of concrete action and operates at the ground level of situational circumstances. A principle is an instruction for how to proceed in applying rules. It addresses the claim among alternatives at a level higher (more abstract) than that of concrete actions – in particular, the choice among alternative rules and principles. And in particular, specific presumptions issue from rules that implement certain basic principles of procedure. The practice at issue, however, is a cognitive practice. One designed for addressing the questions we need to answer is lacking; we must, in the circumstances, settle for a more or less *plausible* one. It is a matter of faute de mieux, of this or nothing (or at any rate nothing better). Presumption is a thought instrumentality that makes it possible for us to do the best we can in circumstances when something must be done. And on this basis, presumption affords yet another instance in which practical considerations play a leading role in our cognitive and communicative practice.

Consider sense perception once more. That we can use the products of our experience of the world to form at least somewhat reliable views of it is the indispensable presupposition of our cognitive endeavors. If we systematically refuse, always and everywhere, to accept *seeming* evidence as *real* evidence (at any rate, until such time as it is discredited), then we can get nowhere in the domain of practical cognition of rational inquiry. When the skeptic rejects any and all presumptions, he automatically blocks the prospect of anyone reasoning with him *within* the standard framework of discussion about the empirical facts of the world.

So what justifies one's making presumptions about factual matters, in the wake of acknowledging that presumptions are not established and certifiable truths? The answer is that presumption is not so much a matter of evidentially *probative* considerations as of procedurally *practical* ones. Presumption is a functional, purpose-serving device. Legal presumptions exist to serve a variety of legal purposes,[3] and epistemic presumptions serve as tools to facilitate the objections for which such cognitive practices as communication and inquiry are instituted. And the validation of a mode of practice is always ultimately pragmatic. Accordingly, even as legal presumptions are validated on the basis of their utility in fostering the aims of the legal enterprise, so cognitive presumptions are validated on the basis of their utility in fostering the aims of the cognitive enterprise – obtaining appropriate answers to our questions and securing useful information. Presumption is, in the end, a practical device whose rationale of validation lies on the order of pragmatic considerations.

The salient factor in validating a presumption is that there is reason to think – and generally experience to show – that in proceeding in this way we fare better than we would otherwise. The justification of these presumptions is not the factual one of the substantive generalization. "In proceeding in this way, you will come at correct information and will not fall into error." Rather, it is methodological justification. In proceeding in this way, you will efficiently foster the interests of

---

[3] See Edmund M. Morgan, "Some Observations Concerning Presumptions," *Harvard Law Review*, 44 (1930–31): 906–34.

the cognitive enterprise; the gains and benefits will, on the whole, outweigh the risks, losses, and costs. Principles of this sort are integral parts of the operational code of agents who transact their cognitive business rationally.

Accordingly, the role of presumption in our cognitive practice is the key. After all, arguments must have premises: *ex nihilo nihil.* We cannot argue everything discursively "all the way down." Here is where presumptions come in. They furnish a starting point. Rational deliberation needs input materials, and principles of presumption provide them. For presumptive facts do not arise discursively. They are given by sources. In matters of sense perception, for example, we presume that mere appearances ("the data") provide an indication of how things actually stand (however imperfect this indication may ultimately prove to be). Viewed in this light, the rational legitimation of a presumptively justified belief lies in the consideration that some generic mode of "purposively favorable indication" speaks on its behalf while no as-yet available counterindication speaks against it.

When, after a careful look, I am under the impression that there is a cat on the mat, I can (quite appropriately) base my acceptance of the contention "There is a cat on the mat" not on certain preestablished premises but simply on my experience – on my visual impression. The salient consideration is that there is no good reason why (in *this* case) I should not indulge my inclination to endorse a visual indication of this kind as veridical. (If there were such evidence – if, for example, I was aware of being in a wax museum – then the situation would, of course, be altered.)

The modus operandi of presumption is a matter of pragmatic efficacy relative to the contextual teleology of the particular enterprise. In criminal law, the root source of presumption, the aim is to convict the guilty while sparing the innocent. And in consequence the usual rules of presumption give them appropriateness. And the same sort of situation obtains throughout this domain.

In communication, for example, the governing principle of the enterprise is to transmit a maximum of information with a minimum of effort. And on this basis we obtain this rule of presumption:

Of alternative constraints of a message you should (unless specifically counterinstructed) always prioritize

- normalcy (the most experience-confirming)
- probability (the most likely)
- simplicity (the least needful of qualification)

And analogously, in matters of inquiry the governing principle is to secure a maximum of reliable, relevant, and usable information. And thus the basis for this rule of presumption:

In answering your questions be guided by such parameters of epistemic reliability as

- evidentiation
- probability
- definiteness (specificity, detail) and such parameters of epistemic utility as
- reliance
- simplicity (economy)
- uniformity (conformity to established cases)

Presumption takes many forms in different contexts; legal presumptions are one thing and epistemic presumptions quite another. And the process of their justification differs accordingly. But the rationale for our principles of presumption is uniformly one and the same: their functional utility in the context at issue. Our policies of presumption are justified through their purposive efficacy in facilitating realization of the inherent purposes and objectives of the domain in which they are instituted. Be it in matters of justice or inquiry or communication, these principles of presumption find their justification, insofar as they indeed are justified, through the common consideration that their operation is pragmatically effective.

There are indeed differences in the ways in which the presumptions of different domains are validated – for example, as between law and ordinary discourse. But these differences all stem from the same underlying source: the specific manifold of purpose that underlies and defines the enterprise at issue. Sometimes – as with the presumptive veracity of sense experience – it is the very practicability of the enterprise at issue that is pivotal; with other enterprises – as with legal presumptions – it is the efficacy of their pursuit that matters. But be it with conditions of possibility or of efficacy, the crux of the matter lies in the functional serviceability of the practice at issue. The point is that throughout all relevant situations, those various familiar principles of presumption exist to further the aims and objectives of the enterprise at hand and the validation of their appropriateness will rest on the issue of their functional serviceability and effectiveness in serving the aims for whose sake they are instituted.

And so the rationale of presumption is ultimately pragmatic. And even specifically cognitive presumption is, in the end, a practical device whose rationale of validation lies on the order of pragmatic considerations. There is, of course, nothing sacrosanct about the result of such a procedure. The choice of the easiest way out may fail us; that which serves adequately at first may not do so in the end. But it is clearly the sensible way to begin. At this elemental level of presumption we proceed by "doing what comes naturally." Specifically, what is fundamental in the cognitive context is the principle of letting appearance be our guide to reality – of accepting the evidence *as evidence* of actual fact, by taking its indications as decisive until such time as suitably weighty counterindications countervail against them. The machinery of presumption is part and parcel of the mechanisms of cognitive rationality because abandoning it would abort the entire project of rational inquiry at the very outset.

3. The Question of Validity

There yet remains a question: Utility is all very good but what of validity? What sorts of considerations *validate* our presumptions? How do they become *entitled* to their favorable epistemic status? The answer has already been foreshadowed. A twofold process is involved. Initially it can be a mere matter of the basic need of a creature whose actions are grounded by thought for answers to its questions. But ultimately we go beyond such this-or-nothing considerations, and the validity of a presumption emerges ex post facto through the utility (both cognitive and practical) of the results it yields. We advance from "this or nothing" to "This or nothing that is determinably better." Legitimation is thus available, albeit only through experiential *retrovalidation*, retrospective validation in the light of eventual experience.[4] It is a

---

[4] See Rescher, *Methodological Pragmatism* (Oxford: Basil Blackwell, 1976) for a fuller development of this line of thought.

matter of learning that a certain issue is more effective in meeting the needs of the situation than its available alternatives. Initially we look to promise and potential but in the end it is applicative efficacy that counts.

At bottom the rationale for presumptions lies in their being critical for the enterprise at hand – in their being somewhere between absolutely necessary and eminently useful. Accordingly, presumptions can root in faute de mieux considerations, though of course the teachings of experience can help, and nothing is as reassuring here as a good track record. The validation of a principle of cognitive presumption can – and ideally should – eventually come to rest on an experiential and evidential foundation. For if it indeed is appropriate in the setting of a certain purposive enterprise to accept the presumptive principle

- in circumstances of type C to presume that P,

then this can and should ultimately rest on the evidentiation of a track record to indicate that in so proceeding we *generally* or *normally* or *ordinarily* promote the realization of this end.

Still, at bottom, the validation of our presumptions is not really theoretical but practical. It does not show that this validation cannot sometimes or often go awry when we endorse the presumptions at issue. Instead it argues only that when we indeed need or want here-and-now to resolve issues and fill informative gaps, then those presumptions represent the most promising ways of doing so, affording us those means to accomplish our goals which – as best we can tell – offer the best prospect of success. Such a line of consideration affords a practical or pragmatic validation in terms of a rational recourse to the optimally available alternative.[5]

And in the end all our presumptions are based on one fundamentally identical rationale of justification, namely, functional efficacy in the particular context of operation in which the presumption figures. To be sure, these contexts will be very different. But as Display 4.1

---

[5] Further detail regarding presumptions and their epistemic role is given in Rescher, *Dialectics* (Albany: State University of New York Press, 1977). The economic aspect of cognition is examined in Rescher, *Cognitive Economy* (Pittsburgh: University of Pittsburgh Press, 1989).

indicates, the ultimately pragmatic character of the justifying considerations is one and the same.

Law: acceptable decisions of legal issues

Human Agency: successful interaction with our fellows in matters of common interest

Communication: effective transfer of information

Inquiry: satisfactory resolution of pressing questions

Science: productive use of factual information in various applications

DISPLAY 4.1. Operative context coordinate telos for the validation of our presumptive practices

---

And so when it comes to the validation of our presumptive practices, the issue is not really one of utility *versus* validity, for the success at issue with utility is itself the best and most telling supportive consideration we can possibly obtain with respect to validity.

Of course, the presumption of innocence in law and the presumption of veracity regarding our senses are very different sorts of measures relating to very difference sorts of matters. But their rationale of justification will take the same structural format, however different their substantive orientations may be.

And so, epistemic presumption, like our cognitive practices in general, has a fundamentally economic rationale in terms of costs and benefits. Like the rest, it too is cost effective within the setting of the project of inquiry to which we stand committed by our place in the world's scheme of things. They are characteristics of the most economical and convenient way for us to secure the data needed to resolve our cognitive problems – to secure answers to our questions about the world we live in. On this basis, we can make ready sense of many of the established rules of information development and management on economic grounds. They prevail because they are maximally cost effective in comparison with the available alternatives.

The validity of a presumption accordingly pivots on two salient considerations: that a contrary presumption would be functionally impracticable, and that presumptive agnosticism would be counterproductive – that factual efficacy in respect to the project at issue would be gravely compromised if that presumption were dispensed with. The first consideration is often best demonstrated by theoretical reflection, the second is generally rendered most vivid by the lessons of experience – by demonstration in practice. Thus what justifies our epistemic presumptions is a combination of utility with demonstrated effectiveness in serving the objectives of the correlative enterprise.

4. How to Assess Success

Suppose some sort of purposive procedure or methodological resource is at issue and that in assessing its adequacy we look to the successes and failures of its application. Two rules of presumption will clearly be operative here

- The method that yields more successes is to be deemed superior.
- The method that yields fewer failures is to be deemed superior.

Odd though it may seem, these two rules of presumption can come into conflict.

Consider that a question can meet with three sorts of responses: a correct answer, an incorrect answer, and no answer at all. A suggestion or recommendation can provide three sorts of guidance: productive guidance that moves matters toward the goal, counterproductive guidance leading away from the goal, or unproductive guidance that moves us neither forward nor back. A medication can be helpful, harmful, or irrelevant. And in just this way any method or measure that we are endearing to approve with respect to its pragmatic utility can prove to be

- successful/helpful/productive
- deleterious/harmful/counterproductive
- nonsuccessful/nonhelpful/(merely) unproductive

Three sorts of outcomes correspondingly lie before us

- successes (moving toward the goal)
- failures (moving away from the goal)
- nonsuccesses (not getting closer to the goal but not dropping back either)

And correspondingly there are two sorts of flaws of deficiencies: the lesser flaws of nonsuccess (or non-gain) and the greater flaws of outright failure (of outright loss).

This distinction of possible flaws in goal-directed behavior has significant implications for pragmatism. For it means that there are in theory two decidedly different standards of pragmatic efficacy. This can be seen as follows.

Consider any sort of goal-directed methodological instrumentality or resource. In seeking to access its track record we must look to the realm of outcomes

> successes (s)
> failures (f)
> and *mere nonsuccesses* that are not actually failures (n)

On this basis, we thus have two potentially different standards of pragmatic efficacy: success maximization and failure minimization; and these will not, in general, come down to the same thing. For to maximize successes is to maximize s. And to minimize failures is to minimize f, or to maximize the sum $s + n$. (Note that standards will come to the same thing only when $n = 0$, that is, only when nonsuccess is seen as constituting failure.) And these two desiderata need by no means be the same. For success maximization calls for maximizing s while failure minimization calls for minimizing f.

For simplicity let us now deal in percentages. And for the sake of an example, consider two different situations:

	A	B
s	60%	70%
f	10%	25%
n	30%	5%

Success maximization favors B, failure minimization favors A. So – which way to go?

The reasonable thing to do is to adopt a combined measure of assessment: success rate × nonfailure rate; in other words:

$$s(s + n)$$

Of course failure minimization comes down to nonfailure maximization – that is, to maximize $100 - f$ (given that we are dealing in percentages). So the most plausible standard for overall maximization would be either a maximization of $s + (100 - f)$ or a maximization of $s \times (100 - f)$. Since $f = 100 - (s + n)$, the former measure comes to $2s + u$ and the second to $s(s + n)$. By the first standard we are to compare for A, $2 \times 60 + 30 = 105$; for B, $2 \times 70 + 5 = 145$. By this final standard A wins out.

With the second standard, matters stand differently. For on this basis our example yields for A, $60 \times 90 = 5400$; for B, $70 \times 75 = 5250$. So A will be the victor here, not withstanding its lower success rate. And this result seems intuitively appropriate.

So we now have three versions of pragmatic preferability:

- success maximization
- failure minimization
- conjoint optimization

And the lesson of the present deliberations is that, in the end, the proper standard of pragmatic assessment would appear to be neither success maximization nor failure minimization but a mode of optimization that embraces the two.

5. The Import of Experience: Avoiding Circularity

On the present approach to cognitive validation, there is no denying that the overall process of justifying our cognitive presumptions is circular. Its structure is as pictured in Display 4.2. The circle here, while only too apparent, is not vicious or vitiating. If the circles close in the right way – so that the rationale of justification meshes properly – then our return to the same place will always be at a *different cognitive level*. What is at issue is thus a pair of distinct but connected cycles (the *theoretical* cycle of cognitive coherence and the *pragmatic* cycle of apparent effectiveness) which both move upward in interlocked coordination – a pair of interlocked ascending spirals. The present approach to epistemic validation finds a "double helix" configuration to lie at the core of human cognition even as it lies at the core of human life itself. The cycle of revalidation moves in a figure 8 configuration. But when we return to "the same place" it is at another epistemic level altogether.[6]

---

[6] There is a question of whether we need to take the view that the cyclic process of revalidation and epistemic upgrading results in "the real truth" by some Peircean process of ultimate convergence. To issue such a guarantee we would either (1) have

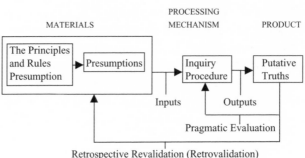

DISPLAY 4.2. The cyclic revalidation of presumptions

And presumptions play an absolutely crucial role here. Some such pre-evidential warrant as is built into the concept of a presumption is clearly needed to avoid vitiating circularity in the justificatory argument under consideration. But nothing vicious ensues if it turns out from the *post-justificatory* standpoint that the thesis whose *antecedent* status is a mere presumption should ultimately acquire the *consequent* status of a truth. And there is nothing fatal if in some instances the consequent status of a "presumptive truth" is actually that of falsehood. For, of course, a rational presumption – unlike an established truth – is defeasible and can turn out to be untrue without undoing its initial status as rationally warranted.

Vicious circularity is thus circumvented thanks to the crucial difference in the utilization of "the same" thesis at different stages – though, to be sure, this difference pertains not to the *assertive content* of the theses used, but to their *epistemic status.*[7]

A principle of presumption does not wear its own validation on its sleeve. As with most any partial resource, the proof of the pudding will be in the eating. The appropriateness of implementing the principle

to redefine truth in the manner of Peirce or (2) adopt a suitably powerful substantive principle to provide an ad hoc guarantee (e.g., a Principle of Limited Variety à la Mill). There is no need for any such desperate remedies, however. One does not have to give any such *constitutive* guarantee of the ultimate effectiveness of our inquiry efforts; it suffices to proceed on the strictly *regulative* basis of a pragmatic assurance that in proceeding as we do we are doing as well as we can possibly manage, being cognitively circumstanced as we are.

7 Further considerations relevant to the ideas of this section are presented in Rescher, *Methodological Pragmatism* (Oxford: Blackwell, 1977).

in this or that case will depend critically on the overall track record of our experience of its use in comparable cases. In these matters of practice, experience can be our guide and teacher. And so it is in the accumulation of a good track record that the induction of such a principle comes to the fore – retrospectively and with the wisdom of hindsight. Put in a nutshell, the legitimation of our principle of presumption is a matter of its *retrovalidation* in the light of experience.

What is at work here is an inductive process. And induction itself is a fundamentality presumptive procedure. Thus the validation of any given policy of presumption will itself rest on presumption of some sort. But there is not vicious circularity here. Certain domains are unavoidably closed with respect to validation. Even as our beliefs can only be rationally substantiated by other beliefs, so our presumptions can without harm be legitimated presumptively.

6. Cultural Evolution as a Teleological Process: Rational Selection

There is every reason to think that the cognitive methods and procedures at issue in the presumptions through which we standardly develop our view of reality evolve selectively by historic, evolutionary process of trial and error – analogous in role to though different in character from the biological mutations affecting the bodily mechanisms by which we comport ourselves in the physical world. An inquiry procedure is an *instrument* for organizing our experience into a systematized view of reality. And as with any tool or method or instrument, the paramount question is, Does it work? Does it produce the desired result? Is it successful in practice in relation to the acquisition and development of information? This sort of legitimation through *rational* selection lies at the basis of the cultural development of our cognitive resources via the variation and selective retention of our epistemically oriented intellectual products.[8]

Given the reasonable agent's well-advised predilection for *success* in one's ventures, the fact that the cognitive methods we employ have a good record of demonstrated effectiveness in regard to explanation,

---

[8] The French school of sociology of knowledge generally envisioned a competition among and natural/rational selection of culturally diverse modes of procedure in accounting for the evolution of logical and scientific thought. Compare Louis Rougier, *Traité de la connaisance* (Paris: Gauthier-Villars, 1955), esp. pp. 426–28.

prediction, and control is not surprising but only to be expected: the community of rational inquirers would have given them up long ago had they not proven to be comparatively successful during a time of random groping – of trial and error. The effectiveness of our cognitive methodology is thus readily accounted for by an evolutionary perspective based on rational selection and the requirements for perpetuation through adoption and transmission.

The historical development of the social processes and practices that characterize the conduct of inquiry affords a clear illustration of this phenomenon of rational selection. In any community of interacting rational agents, the pragmatic impetus conduces powerfully to the selection and retention of those practices that prove themselves to be teleologically successful and functionally cost-effective in realizing the shared aims of the enterprise at hand. And in particular, the development of our standard epistemic usages and procedures can best be understood on this basis.

It is thus not difficult to give examples of the operation of evolutionary processes relating to presumptions in the cognitive domain. The intellectual landscape of human history is littered with the skeletal remains of the extinct dinosaurs of this sphere. Examples of such defunct methods for the acquisition and explanatory utilization of information include astrology, numerology, oracles, dream interpretation, the reading of tea leaves or the entrails of birds, animism, the teleological physics of the pre-Socratic thinkers, and so on. No doubt, such practices continue in operation in some human communities to this very day, but clearly not among those dedicated to serious inquiry into nature's ways – that is, scientists. There is nothing intrinsically absurd or inherently contemptible about such unorthodox cognitive programs – even the most occult of them have a long and not wholly unsuccessful history. (Think, for example, of the prominent role of numerological explanation from Pythagoreanism, through Platonism, to the medieval Arabs, down to Kepler in the Renaissance.) Distinctly different scientific methodologies and programs have been mooted: Ptolemaic "saving the phenomena" versus the hypothetico-deductive method, or Baconian collectionism versus the post-Newtonian theory of experimental science. The emergence, development, and subsequent triumph of our ultimately established methods of inquiry and explanation invite an evolutionary account, though clearly one that involves rational rather than natural selection. And the cognitive methods in which our standard policies of presumption are embedded are part and parcel of this.

Overall, two sorts of evolutionary pressures are at work in relation to cognitive matters. First there is the biological (Darwinian) pressure of *natural* selection of mechanisms that prove biologically effective in meeting needs. Second there is the epistemic (Lamarckian) pressure of *rational* selection of procedures that prove experimentally effective in this direction. And between the two the course of historical development itself reflects the unfolding of a validating rationale for our standard cognitive practices. Accordingly, an individual's heritage comes from two main sources: a biological heritage derived from the parents and a cultural heritage derived from the society. However, in the development of our knowledge, this second factor becomes critical. To establish and perpetuate itself in any community of *rational* agents, a practice or method of procedure must prove itself in the course of experience. Not only must it be to some extent effective in realizing the pertinent aims and ends, but it must prove itself to be more efficient than a comparably available alternative. With societies composed of rational agents, the pressure of means-end efficacy is ever at work in forging a process of cultural (rather than natural) selection for replacing less by more cost-effective ways of achieving the group's committed ends – its cognitive ends emphatically included. Our cognitive faculties are doubtless the product of biological evolution, but the processes and procedures by which we put them to work are the results of a *cultural* evolution that proceeds through rationally guided trial and error in circumstances of a pragmatic preference for retaining those processes and procedures that prove theorists efficient and effective.[9] Rational people have a strong bias for what works. And progress is swift because once rationality gains an inch, it takes a mile. Of course, cultural evolution is shaped and canalized by constraints that themselves are the products of biological evolution, for our instincts, inclinations, and natural dispositions are all programmed

[9] These present deliberations have a close kinship with the "epigenetic rules" that figure prominently in Michael Ruse's *Taking Darwin Seriously* (Oxford: Blackwell, 1986). The only significant divergence is that Ruse sees the rules at issue as having a predominantly biological basis, where as the present discussion sees their basis as predominantly cultural.

into us by evolution. The transition from a biologically advantageous economy of effective physical effort to a cognitively advantageous economy of effective intellectual efforts is a short and easy step.

The point here is that all our cognitive methods and procedures – the instrumentality of presumption prominently included – are the products of developmental emergence through cultural selection that reflects a track record of success. Their validation inheres in their operation – they develop as they do because they substantially succeed in their intended role. Their very existence indicates their efficacy and betokens a confluence of history and pragmatism, for in matters of rational selection the developmental process powerfully betokens justificatory validation.[10]

A brief summary of this chapter's somewhat convoluted argumentation is in order. The rational validation of presumptions that has been maintained here lies in the following consideration:

- Particular presumptions are always grounded in general rules that themselves reflect broader principles.
- These principles provide for a general practice based on a cognitive policy.
- Since there are many sorts of purposive contexts with varying ends in view, there will be many different ways of justifying presumptions. But the format of cognitive justification – its generic structure – is always the same: a matter of purposive efficacy in the particular context at issue.
- Cognitive policies of procedures – and the principles and rules that implement them – came to be validated on the same essentially pragmatic and economic grounds of functional effectiveness as in any other *modus operandi*.
- Rational selection on the basis of factual efficacy and effectiveness affords telling substantiation for such purposively instantiated methodological resources.

In the context of the cognitive practices of intelligent beings whose actions are governed by their beliefs – those practices relating to

[10] For further details regarding some of the relevant issues see Rescher, *A Useful Inheritance* (Savage, Md.: Rowman and Littlefield, 1990).

presumption included – rational selection and epistemic validation proceed hand-in-hand.

Initially we do or should proceed subject to the consideration that the practice at issue is goal-facilitative: that its adoption is prima facie conducive to the realization of certain of our cognitive objectives. And then *ultimately* we do or should have the backing of retrospective revalidation via the (essentially inductive) support of the consideration that in adopting this practice on various occasions in the past we succeeded in realizing the objectives at issue. Therefore, the proceedings at issue are a retrovalidation via a supportive track record of applicative success and functional efficacy in matters of practice. Underlying our subscription to presumptions is something that itself has the status of a cardinal mega-presumption of procedural rationality, namely, that the rationally appropriate and optimal way to handle a particular case is to resolve it under the aegis of those general processes of procedure that have worked before. To reemphasize: justificatory rationale of our presumptive practice is in the end pragmatic. There being many different contexts of presumption, there will be many different procedures of validating presumption rather than one single all-inclusive justification. But the process of justification – the way of going at it – is always one and the same: pragmatic efficacy in regard to the functional/purposive teleology of the particular domain at issue.

And given the pragmatic justification of our presumptions, the domain of epistemic presumption is a crossroad where considerations of practical and theoretical reason intersect. Those epistemic presumptions are, in effect, practical policies justified by their serviceability in the furtherance of our cognitive interests.

5

Presumption and Inquiry

1. Presumptions in Rational Inquiry

Without *some* recourse to presumption we simply could not manage to obtain the informative inputs indispensable for answering our questions about factual issues. Some degree of presumption (however small) incredibly attaches to our procedurally validated truths throughout the factual area where defeasibility is virtually inescapable. This becomes clear once one considers the issue of the observational *inputs* essential to inquiry in the factual domain. If *their* status always had to be that of established truths, we could never get off the ground, since observational experience just does not work like that. Thus if an "ordinary process of inferential reasoning" were at issue here, we would be in deep trouble as any such process can only extract truths *from truths*, and if the inputs themselves had to be established truths, the whole process would be vitiated at the outset. Happily this is not so. An inquiry procedure is clearly not an "ordinary process of inference": it must afford an *originative* mechanism, capable of yielding an output of (putative) truths without demanding an initial input of previously established (putative) truths. Clearly if we hewed to the line that rationally discursive procedures can only extract truths from truths, we would be offered the unattractive choice between (1) accepting a "starter set" of nondiscursively self-evident or self-validating truths, or (2) a skepticism that admits defeat and gives up the whole project of a rational validation of truth-acceptance. This dilemma can be addressed effectively by resorting to presumptions. And so presumption represents a crucial epistemological resource that one would have to make room for in any case, even if it did not afford so convenient a filler for informational gaps.

Accordingly, a policy of presumption can play a crucial role in inquiry by furnishing us with materials for answering our questions.[1] And on grounds of cognitive economy, presumption favors the usual and the natural – its tendency is one of convenience and ease of operation in cognitive affairs. And there is nothing sacrosanct about the result of such a procedure. Extracting ourselves from perplexity by following the easiest and most convenient way out may fail us; that which serves adequately in the first analysis may no longer do so in the end. But it is clearly the sensible way to begin.

But is a recourse to presumption not itself caught up in an infinite regress of substantiation? If a presumption requires a rationale and that rationale itself requires a grounding to establish its appropriateness as such, then are we not in automatic difficulty? Not really! For that rationale need not itself be epistemic in character: it can be practical. It can rely not on positive evidentiation but on mere faute de mieux considerations. With presumptions in place, probative considerations of efficacy can come ex post facto: they need not come in advance.

On this basis, then, we proceed via truth estimates initially provided by principles of presumption that are ultimately reevaluated on the basis of experience, as per the picture of Display 5.1. An inquiry procedure having this overall structure escapes the vitiating cycle of basing truth-claims solely upon prior truth-claims, and does so without appeal to a problematic category of self-certifying truths.

The process of presumption in matters of inquiry is illustrated by rules on the order of those listed in Display 5.2. Eventually these are retrovalidated – retrospectively revalidated (ex post facto) by the results of that inquiry. But at this later stage their epistemic status – though not their *content* – changes. *In the first instance* these presumptions have a merely provisional and regulative standing. But in the sequel they can attain a suitable degree of factual/constitutive

---

[1] This is why adherence to custom is a cardinal principle of cognitive as well as practical rationality. Cf. William James, "The Sentiment of Rationality" in *The Will to Believe and Other Essays in Popular Philosophy* (New York: Longmans Green, 1897).

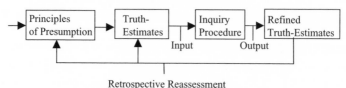

Retrospective Reassessment

DISPLAY 5.1. Inquiry as an input-output process

- To trust in the evidence of one's senses and in the reliability of the customary sources of information in general
- To proceed on the principle that what seems to be is
- To answer one's questions on the basis of the best available evidence; to accept the conclusions supported by the strongest arguments
- To explain people's actions via rationality; to bow to the view people are rational and do what they do for what seem to them to be good reasons

DISPLAY 5.2. Some rules of presumption in rational inquiry

substantiation through a course of cognitive development moving from the very tentative to the very secure.

For an example, consider the evidential presumption of trusting the relevant information that is available to us. This involves two issues. First, that of rational credibility – namely, when there is some evidence (albeit weak) that something is so and no indications whatsoever to the contrary, then we can and should presume it to be so. (Hence, H. M. Stanley's "Dr. Livingston, I presume.") The second is the presumption in favor of the alternative that enjoys the preponderance of evidence, where the strength of presumption is clearly in line with the matter of evidential weight. Presumption thus figures in rational inquiry as a key element in a dynamic process of knowledge acquisition.

2. Presumption and the Diallelus

It is instructive to contemplate a line of reasoning regarding man's prospects of attaining knowledge about the world that has been known from the days of the skeptics of antiquity under the title of the "*diallelus*" (*ho diallêlos tropos*) – or "the wheel" – which presents a particular sort of vicious-circle argumentations (*circulus vitiosus in probandi*).² Montaigne presented this Wheel Argument, as we may term it, as follows:

To adjudicate [between the true and the false] among the appearances of things we need to have a distinguishing method (*un instrument judicatoire*); to validate this method we need to have a justifying argument; but to validate this justifying argument we need the very method at issue. And there we are, going round on the wheel.³

The classical formulation of the argument comes from Sextus Empiricus:

[I]n order to decide the dispute which has arisen about the criterion we must possess an accepted criterion by which we shall be able to judge the dispute; and in order to possess an accepted criterion, the dispute about the criterion must first be decided. And when the argument thus reduces itself to a form of circular reasoning (*diallêlus*), the discovery of the criterion becomes impracticable, since we do not allow them to adopt a criterion by assumption, while if they offer to judge the criterion by a criterion we force them to a regress *ad infinitum*. And furthermore, since demonstration requires a demonstrated criterion, while the criterion requires an approved demonstration, they are forced into circular reasoning.⁴

In sum, it would be futile to address the question of the adequacy of our mechanisms of knowledge acquisition in terms of their capacity to deliver the actual truth.

The point of this line of thought is precisely that this would be viciously circular, since we have no independent access to "the truth" as such. What we must do in rational inquiry is pull ourselves up by our own bootstraps, relying on our principles of presumption but critically

---

² On this argument see Roderick M. Chisholm, *The Problem of the Criterion* (Milwaukee: Marquette University Press, 1973).

³ "Pour juger des appearances que nous recevons des subjects, il nous faudroit un instrument judicatoire; pour verifier cet instrument, il nous fault de la démonstration; pour verifier la démonstration, un instrument: nous voilà au rouet." *Essaies*, Bk. II, ch. 12 ("An Apologie of Raymond Second"), p. 544 of the Modern Library edition of *The Essays of Montaigne* (New York: The Modern Library, 1933). Francis Bacon, with the characteristic shrewdness of a lawyer, even managed to turn the *diallelus* into a dialectical weapon against his methodological opponents: "no judgment can be rightly formed either of my method, or of the discoveries to which it leads, by means of . . . the reasoning which is now in use, since one cannot postulate due jurisdiction for a tribunal which is itself on trial" (*Novum Organon*, Bk. I, sect. 33).

⁴ *Outlines of Pyrrhonism*, Bk. II, sect. 20 (tr. R. G. Bury) (Cambridge, Mass.: Harvard University Press, 1933 [Loeb Classical Library]); compare Bk. I, sects. 114–17. See also the article on Pyrrho in Bayle's *Dictionary*.

reappraising them as well. We begin by provisionally accepting certain theses whose initial status is not that of certified truths at all, but merely that of plausible postulations, whose role in inquiry is (at this stage) one of regulative facilitation.

It is difficult to exaggerate the significance of this extremely simple line of reasoning, which sets the stage for the skeptic's criterion argument to the effect that an adequate standard of knowledge can never be secured. For the ancient skeptics – who originated this argument – sought to use it to enmesh in absurdity their Stoic opponents, who advocated a certain criterion of truth. The skeptics argued (in effect):

Quis custodiet ipsos custodes? How are you going to validate your criterion itself? Surely not on its own ground, in terms of itself? That's just begging the question. In terms of another? But that just starts an infinite regress – like the ancient myth about supporting the earth on the back of an elephant, and this on the back of an alligator, and so on. The choice before you is an unattractive one – that between a vicious circle or a vitiating regress. Either way, you have no adequate means to support the truth-criterion which lies at the foundation of your cognitive enterprise.

The logical structure of this justificatory process incorporates a feedback loop leading from the truths validated by the inquiry procedure back to the initial "merely presumptive" truths, so that the appropriateness of these initial, tentative, merely plausible presumptions can be reassessed.

And of course, matters need not always go smoothly. For one thing, this process clearly makes retrospective reevaluation possible, and here the outputs can bite the input-providing hand that feeds them, in due course rejecting some inputs as false. An initial presumption may well drop by the wayside in the long run. It is only normal and to be expected that this should happen, given the merely tentative probative nature of presumptions. But if it happens systematically rather than sporadically – if presumptions generally turned out false in this light of hindsight – then something would have gone seriously amiss. (But one could, without problems, invalidate an entire source that has provided a basis of presumptions, as is shown by the example of abandonment of the long-standing practice of giving probative weight to dreams, omens, signs, portents, etc.)

This points toward a cyclic process of revalidation and cognitive upgrading in the course of which presumptive theses used as inputs for the inquiry procedure come to acquire by gradual stages an enhanced epistemic status. The structure of this retrospective revalidation of *inputs* is precisely the same as that already considered for the revalidation of the metaphysical basis of cognitive legitimation as set out in the preceding discussion.

3. Presumption and the Contrast between Foundationalism and Coherentism

A presumption-based, coherentist theory of knowledge stands in sharp contrast with the more restrictive foundationalist approach of the mainstream tradition of Western epistemology. For coherentism, unlike foundationalism, dispenses with any appeal to basic, immediately apprehensible truths of fact. It abandons the view that knowledge of the actual – or indeed even of the probable – requires a foundation of certainty. Instead, it takes the stance that truth is accessible in the extralogical realm on the basis of considerations of systemic best-fit among mere truth-presumptions, and thereby without any foundation of certainty. (The qualifier "factual" occurs here because the instrumental need for the resources of logic is, of course, conceded, seeing that they are needed as a mechanism for best-fit judgments, since logic must be used in determining what does and does not "fit.") This entire procedure goes wholly counter to the classical epistemologists' problematic and ultimately futile quest for basic or foundational truths regarding factual matters. For the difficulty with any sort of foundationalism lies in the matter of foundations. If they are phenomenal ("I seem to see a steel dagger before me," "I deem it highly likely that he will come") then they are autobiographical rather than objectively factual. If, on the other hand, they are factual ("There is an apple on the table" – which, of course, cannot have a golden interior; after all, apples just don't, even though I have not checked this), then it is hard to see how they can be foundational, since their own status is problematic.[5]

---

[5] When I presented such a critique of foundationalism in discussion some time ago, an interlocutor reproved me for not crediting these ideas to my late colleague Wilfred

The foundationalist approach to factual knowledge thus faces a dilemma: the sort of claims at issue in objective knowledge lack cognitively unproblematic foundations, while cognitively unproblematic contentions do not yield objective facts. Coherentism sets out to resolve this problem. Rather than proceeding linearly, by fresh deductions from several premises, it proposes to cycle round and round the same given family of prospects and possibilities, sorting out, refitting, refining until a more sophisticatedly developed and more deeply elaborated resolution is ultimately arrived at. The information-extracting process developed along these lines is one not of advance into new informative territory, but one of a cyclic reappraisal and revision of the old, tightening the net around our ultimate conclusion as we move round and round again, gaining a surer confidence in the wake of more refined reappraisals. However there must be a starting point.

The concept of a *datum*, whose role is pivotal in coherentist methodology, is something of a technical innovation. To be sure, the idea is one not *entirely* unrelated to the ordinary use of that term, nor to its (somewhat different) use among philosophers; yet it is significantly different from both. A datum is a *truth-candidate*, a proposition to be taken not as true, but as potentially or *presumptively* true. It is a *prima facie* truth in exactly the sense in which one speaks of *prima facie* duties in ethics – a thesis that we would in the circumstances, be prepared to class as true provided that no countervailing considerations are operative. A datum is thus a proposition that one is to class as true *if one can*, that is, if doing so does not generate any difficulties or inconsistencies.

4. Coherentism and the Evidential Grounding of Claims to Truth

In his exposition of the coherence theory, Brand Blanshard has written:

Granting that propositions, to be true, must be coherent with each other, may they not be coherent without being true?...Again, a novel, or a succession

---

Sellars on the basis of his paper, "Giveness and Explanatory Coherence" (*Journal of Philosophy*, 70 [1973]). They were, however, developed quite independently and figured already in my book *The Coherence Theory of Truth* (Oxford: Clarendon Press, 1973), which went off to the printer well before Wilfred's paper was published.

of novels such as Galsworthy's *Forsyte Saga,* may create a special world of characters and events which is at once extremely complex and internally consistent; does that make it the less fictitious? ... This objection, like so many other annihilating criticisms, would have more point if anyone had ever held the theory it demolishes. But if intended to represent the coherence theory as responsibly advocated, it is a gross misunderstanding. That theory does not hold that any and every system is true, no matter how abstract and limited; it holds that one system only is true, namely the system in which everything real and possible is coherently included. How one can find in this the notion that a system would still give truth if, like some arbitrary geometry, it disregarded experience completely, it is not easy to see.[6]

Blanshard's position is at bottom correct. The coherence theory would indeed be deficient if it held "that a system would still give truth if ... it disregarded experience completely." Our recourse to *data* in the presently operative provisional sense is intended to supply just this requisite of a recourse to "experience."

Such a datum is – in the traditional sense – a "given." But of course it is given not as an authentic truth but only as a *truth-candidate,* as *potentially* or *presumptively* true; to be classed as true provided that doing so creates no anomalies. When "given" on this basis, a presumption is a provisional estimate that represents our most plausible *candidate* for truth whose credentials may well prove insufficient, a runner in a race it may not win. As far as its correctness goes, a presumption is accordingly less a *given* than a *taken.*

For a proposition to count as such a datum is altogether different from its counting as a truth, just as a man's being a presidential candidate is something far different from his being a president. Presidential candidates are not presidents; data are not truths. Truth-candidacy does not require or presuppose truth: quite different issues are involved. A potential truth is a truth no more than an egg-enclosed embryo is a hen. The "acceptance" of a proposition as a truth-candidate is not *acceptance* at all but a highly provisional and conditional epistemic *inclination* toward it, an inclination that falls far short of outright commitment. A datum is not *established* as true; it is backed only by a *presumption* that it may turn out true "if all goes well." It lays a claim to truth, but it may not be able to make good this claim. To assert *P*

---

[6] Brand Blanshard, *The Nature of Thought* (London: Macmillan, 1939), pp. 275–6.

as a datum is to say no more than that *P* is *potentially* or *presumptively* true – that it is a truth-candidate – but does not say that *P* is *actually* true, that it is a truth. As with assertions of possibility or probability, a claim of datahood definitely stops short – far short – of a claim to truth. To reemphasize: in the context of truth, a datum or "given" effectively figures as a *taken*.

The *presumptive* standing of such a datum means that this conception certainly does not "open the floodgates" in an indiscriminate way. Not *everything* is a datum: the concept is to have *some* logico-epistemic bite. To be a datum is not just to be a proposition that *could conceivably* be claimed to be true but to be a proposition that (under the circumstances) can be claimed to be true with at least *some* plausibility: its claim must be well founded. A proposition will not qualify as a datum without *some* appropriate grounding. Data are propositions that have a proper claim upon truth, and we must distinguish between truth-claims that can reasonably be made from those that are merely theoretically possible. (Not every human being is a possible winner in a race but only those who are genuinely "in the running.") So understood, a datum is a proposition which, given the circumstances of the case, is a *real prospect for truth* in terms of the availability of reasons to warrant its truth-candidacy. A datum is a mere guess. It is not just something that is "possibly true" or that is "true for all I know about the matter." To class a proposition as a datum is to take a definite and presumptively committal position with respect to it, so as to say "I propose to accept it as true in so far as this is permitted by analogous and possibly conflicting commitments elsewhere." A datum, in sum, is a bearer of presumption.

It is sometimes objected that coherentism cannot be the standard of truth because there we may well arrive at a multiplicity of diverse but equally coherent structures, whereas truth is of its very nature conceived of as unique and monolithic. Bertrand Russell, for one, has argued in this way:

There is no reason to suppose that only *one* coherent body of beliefs is possible. It may be that, with sufficient imagination, a novelist might invent a past for the world that would perfectly fit on to what we know, and yet be quite different from the real past. In more scientific matters, it is certain that there are often two or more hypotheses which account for all the known facts on some subject, and although, in such cases, men of science endeavour to find facts which will rule out all the hypotheses except one, there is no reason why they should always succeed.[7]

One must certainly grant Russell's central point: there is something fundamentally undiscriminating about coherence of and by itself. Coherence may well be – nay certainly is – a descriptive feature of the domain of truths: they cohere. But there is nothing in this to prevent propositions other than truths from cohering with one another: fiction can be made as coherent as fact: truths surely have no monopoly of coherence. Indeed "it is logically possible to have two different but equally comprehensive sets of coherent statements between which there would be, in the coherence theory, no way to decide which was the set of true statements."[8] In consequence, coherence alone cannot

---

[7] Bertrand Russell, *The Problems of Philosophy* (New York: H. Holt, 1912), p. 191. Or compare Moritz Schlick's formulation of this point: "Since no one dreams of holding the statements of a story book true and those of a text of physics false, the coherence view fails utterly. Something more, that is, must be added to coherence, namely, a principle in terms of which the compatibility is to be established [sc. as factual], and this would alone then be the actual criterion" (M. Schlick, "The Foundation of Knowledge," in A. J. Ayer [ed.], *Logical Positivism* [Glencoe, Ill.: The Free Press, 1959], pp. 209–27 [see p. 216]).

[8] A. R. White, "Coherence Theory of Truth" in P. Edward (ed.), *The Encyclopedia of Philosophy*, Vol. 2 (1967), pp. 130–3 (see p. 131). One critic of the coherence theory elaborates this important point with demonstrative clarity as follows: "That in the end only one sufficiently comprehensive system of statements would be found consistent, is a suggestion which runs counter to obvious facts about the nature of consistency and of systems; probably it strikes us as plausible because we are such poor liars, and are fairly certain to become entangled in inconsistencies sooner or later, once we depart from the truth. A sufficiently magnificent liar, however, or one who was given time and patiently followed a few simple rules of logic, could eventually present us with any number of systems, as comprehensive as you please, and all of them including falsehoods. Insofar as it is possible to deal with any such notion as 'the whole of the truth', it is the Leibnizian conception of an infinite plurality of possible worlds which is justified, and not the conception of the historical coherence theory that there is just one all-comprehensive system, uniquely determined to be true by its complete consistency.... Thus if we start with any empirical [i.e., contingent] belief or statement 'P', we shall find that one or other of every pair of further empirical statements, 'Q' and 'not-Q', 'R' and 'not-R', etc., can be conjoined with 'P' to form a self-consistent set. And exactly the same will likewise be true of its contradictory 'not-P'. *Every empirical supposition, being a contingent statement, is contained in some self-consistent system which is as comprehensive as you please.* And as between the truth of any empirical belief or statement 'P' and the falsity of it (the truth of 'not-P') consistency with other possible beliefs or statements, or inclusion in comprehensive and self-consistent systems, provides no clue or basis of decision" (C. I. Lewis, *An Analysis of Knowledge and Valuation* [La Salle, Ill.: Carus Publishing, 1962], pp. 340–1).

discriminate between truths and falsehoods. But of course no one has
said that it could. What coherentists have always insisted on is coherence *with the data of experience.* The coherence at issue here is not just a
matter of coherence among propositions (no further questions asked)
but coherence among the data (the *presumptively* true propositions).
It looks not to coherence in and of itself as a criterion of truth, but to
coherence with the data of experience. It thus renders a Russell-type
objection beside the point.

After all, coherence must always be coherence *with* something: the
phrase "to cohere with" requires an object just as much as "to agree
with" does. We do not really have a coherence theory in hand at all,
until the *target domain* of coherence is specified. And it must be said in
defense of the traditional coherence theorists that they insisted that
for them it is not free-floatingly unqualified coherence but specifically "coherence with our experience" that is to be the standard of
truth.[9] The coherence theory of the British idealists has never abandoned altogether the empiricist tendency of the native tradition of
philosophy.

And so, the concept of plausible data performs a critically important
job for the coherence theory of truth. It serves to provide an answer to
the question "Coherent with what?" without postulating a prior category of fundamental truth. It provides the coherence theory with grist
for its mill that need not itself be the product of some preliminary
determination of truth. A reliance upon data as merely presumptive
truths makes it possible to contemplate a coherence theory that pro-
duces its truth claims not *ex nihilo* (which would be impossible) but yet
from a basis that does not itself demand any prior determinations of
truthfulness as such. A coherence criterion can, on this basis, furnish
a mechanism that is *originative* of truth – that is, it yields truths – via

---

[9] See A. C. Ewing, *Idealism: A Critical Survey* (London: Macmillan, 1934), p. 238, as well
as his later essay on "The Correspondence Theory of Truth" where he writes: "that
coherence is the test of truth can only be made plausible if coherence is interpreted
not as mere internal coherence but as coherence with our experience" (*Non-Linguistic
Philosophy* [London: Allen & Unwin, 1968], pp. 203–4). For an author of the earlier
period, see H. H. Joachim who writes: "Truth, we said, was the systematic coherence
which characterized a significant whole. And we proceeded to identify a significant
whole with 'an organized individual experience, self-filling and self-fulfilled'" (*The
Nature of Truth* [Oxford: Clarendon Press, 1906], p. 78).

presumptions that yield (putatively) true outputs without requiring that truths must also be present among the supplied inputs. In making this mechanism work, the idea of presumption plays a crucially important role in theoretical epistemology.[10]

---

[10] Further detail regarding the coherence theory of truth can be found in my work of this title (Oxford: Clarendon Press, 1973).

6

Default Reasoning

1. Default Inference

The topic of default reasoning also affords instructive insights into the nature of presumptions. A *default* in logic is a fall-back position in point of conclusion-drawing – one to which we can appropriately resort when circumstances prove uncooperative. But of course things ought not to go wrong in logic. So what is going on here?

Orthodox inferential reasoning proceeds via *logically valid* inference processes which do – and must – proceed from true premises to true conclusions. They review the inherent connections coming actually or assumptively accepted commitments. Logic functions within the limits of the given. By contrast, default reasoning – which involves an information gap between premises and conclusion – goes beyond this into uncharted territories. In consequence, plausible (though sometimes false) premises will lead to plausible (though possibly false) conclusions.

The logical validity of inference rules in standard (truth-functional) logic is determined on an input-output basis, a valid rule being one that will invariably yield true outputs (conclusions) from true inputs (premises). All such inference rules will faithfully and unfailingly transmit the truth of premises to the conclusions. By contrast, the inference processes of default logic are such that the truth – real or suppositional – of the premises does not assure the truth of the conclusion but will at most establish that conclusion as contextually plausible.

Such inferences are *ampliative*: the conclusion can go beyond what the premises guarantee. And this means that such reasonings are fallible and can – and occasionally will – lead from truth to falsity.

We shall represent *logically valid deducibility* (in its classical construction) by ⊢, and shall by contrast use ⊪ to represent the *plausible inferability* at issue with default reasoning. And there is a significant difference here. Logic and reference by inference: it tells you what to say when the circumstances *mandate* it. Default, by contrast, is presumptive: it tells you what to say when the circumstances *permit* it – that is, in the absence of case-specific counterindications.[1]

Some examples of inference-processes in default logic are as follows:

1. *p* is highly likely ⊪ *p*.
2. *p* is very likely, *q* is very likely, ⊪ *p* & *q* is very likely.
3. There is strong evidence in favor of *p* and no more than weak evidence against it ⊪ *p*.
4. *p* has obtained in all past instances, ⊪ *p* will obtain in the next instance.

As these examples indicate, the inference processes of default reasoning can all be assimilated to an inferential pattern of the following generic structure (which does clearly obtain as valid in traditional logic):

- In all ordinary (normal, standard, commonplace) cases, whenever *p*, then *q*.
- *p* obtains in the case presently at hand.
- < The present case is an ordinary (normal, standard, etc.) one.>
∴ *q* obtains in the present case.

Clearly, that third, usually tacit and thereby enthymematic, premise plays a pivotal role here. And it is, in general, able to do so not because we have secured it as a certified truth, but simply because it is a plausible (albeit defeasible) presumption that is strongly supported by the

---

[1] By extension the terminology of default is also such in the context of control theory. Here a device is said to default to a certain (circumstantially "normal") condition if it takes on this condition whenever the explicit instructions of its situation do not require otherwise.

available evidence – though not, of course, guaranteed. Default reasoning thus rests on arguments that would be valid if all of their premises – explicit and tacit alike – were authentic truths, which they are not since at least one of the critical premises of the argument is no more than a mere presumption. Accordingly, default inference is *reasoning that is enthymematically based on a plausible presumption*. And the *defeasible presumption* that is at issue here is emphatically not to be regarded as an established truth but merely something that holds only provisionally, as long as is no counterindicatively conflicting information comes to light.

Against this background, the procedure that is definitively characteristic of default reasoning is this:

To treat what is generally (normally, standardly, generally, usually, etc.) the case *as if* it were the case always and everywhere, and thereby applicable in the present instance.

One salient policy of rational procedure may be characterized as that of a *presumption of adequacy*: the principle that the best we can manage at the moment is good enough: that if and when we must choose, then we are entitled to rest satisfied with the best we can manage at the time. Of course, no one believes it to be a matter of sound general principle that what appears best at the time is good enough. But it is nevertheless sensible to act on this basis (if act we must). And this general policy has obvious epidemic consequences. It means that if and when there is reason to resolve a question one way or the other, then we should do so on the basis of what – at the time – appears to be in line with the best (i.e., strongest) reasons.

On this basis a default is a thesis which, as a matter of policy, stands as acceptable unless there is some overt reason to think otherwise – a thesis that is acceptable faute de mieux on grounds of principle. Default reasoning represents an economy of processes: it reflects a policy to go forward with what we have in hand on the most economical basis. Here ignorance is bliss: where there is no good reason to see the case at hand as being out of the ordinary, we simply presume it to be an ordinary one in the absence of visible counterindications. Such a practice is in effect a *principle of presumption* that what generally holds also holds in the case at hand. This stance is part of the core modus operandi of default reasoning.[2]

2. Facing the Prospect of Error

Of course our presumptions, however plausible, can go awry, for the situation at hand may not be standard and representative as the enthymematic comportment of the argument requires. This is brought out vividly in John Godfry Saxe's poem "The Blind Men and the Elephant," which tells the story of certain blind sages, those "six men of Indostan / To learning much inclined / Who went to see the elephant / (Though all of them were blind)." One sage touched the elephant's "broad and sturdy side" and declared the beast to be "very like a wall." The second, who had felt its tusk, announced the elephant to resemble a spear. The third, who took the elephant's squirming trunk in his hands, compared it to a snake; while the fourth, who put his arm around the elephant's knee, was sure that the animal resembled a tree. A flapping ear convinced another that the elephant had the form of a fan; while the sixth blind man thought that it had the form of a rope, since he had taken hold of the tail.

> And so these men of Indostan,
> Disputed loud and long;
> Each in his own opinion
> Exceeding stiff and strong:
> Though each was partly in the right,
> And all were in the wrong.

[2] Default reasoning plays a significant role in the theory of reasoning and also in artificial intelligence. On the topic and its ramifications see "Common-Sense Reasoning" in *The Routledge Encyclopedia of Philosophy* (London: Routledge, 2000) and Robert E. Mercer, *A Default-Logic Approach to Natural Language Persupposition* (Vancouver: University of British Columbia, 1987). See also Nicholas Rescher, *Plausible Reasoning* (Assen: Van Gorcum, 1976), and Rescher, *Induction* (Oxford: Basil Blackwell, 1980); Raymond Reiter, "A Logic for Default Reasoning," *Artificial Intelligence*, 13 (1980): 81–132; William L. Harper, "A Sketch of Some Recent Developments in the Theory of Conditionals," in W. L. Harper, L. G. Pearson, and R. Stalnaker (eds.), *IFS: Conditionals, Belief, Decision, Chance and Time* (Dordrecht: D. Reidel, 1981); Kent Bach, "Default Reasoning," *Pacific Philosophical Quarterly*, 65 (1984): 37–58; J. L. Pollock, "A Theory of Defeasible Reasoning," *International Journal of Intelligent Systems*, 6 (1991): 33–54; and Henry E. Kyburg, Jr., and Chon Man Teng, *Uncertain Inference* (Cambridge: Cambridge University Press, 2001).

None of those blind sages was altogether in error; it is just that the facts at their disposal were nontypical and unrepresentative in a way that gave them a biased and misleading picture of the actual facts. It is not that they did not know truth, but rather that an altogether plausible inference from the partial truth they knew propelled them into overall error.

But if such a policy of typicality presumption may lead us down the primrose path of error, how is it ever to be justified? The answer here lies precisely in the consideration that what is at issue is not a truth-claim but a policy or procedure. And such policies of procedure are not justified in the theoretical (i.e., factual) order but in the practical or pragmatic order of deliberation. The validation at issue runs roughly as follows:

1. We have questions to which we need a (satisfactory) answer, and in the face of this we take the stance that . . .
2. We are rationally entitled to use a premise that holds good promise of finding an answer (i.e., is effective or more effective than the other available alternatives), even though it may occasionally fail.

On this basis we proceed, subject to the idea that if and when things go wrong, this is a bridge we can cross when we get there, invoking "explanations" and excuses to indicate the unusual (anormal, extraordinary) circumstances of the case.

Even as in real life we cannot manage our affairs sensibly without running risks, so in the cognitive life one must, on occasion, take the risk of error in stride, since the inevitable result of a radical nothing-risk policy is the nothing-have of radical skepticism. And this situation is particularly prominent in inductive contexts.

3. Induction as Default Reasoning

The term *induction* is derived from the Latin rendering of Aristotle's *epagôgê* – the process for inferring to a generalization from its specific instances.[3] Gradually extended over an increasingly wide range,

---

3 See W. D. Ross, *Aristotle's Prime and Posterior Analytics* (Oxford: Clarendon Press, 1949), pp. 47–51.

induction can be seen as a question-answering device encompassing virtually the whole range of nondeductive reasoning. Thus consider a typical inductive argument – that from "All the magnets we have examined attract iron filings" to "All magnets attract iron filings." It would be deeply problematic to regard this as a deductive argument that rests on the (obviously false) premise: "What is the case in all examined instances is universally the case." Rather, what we have here is a plausible presumption that takes the cases in hand to be typical and generally representative in the absence of concrete counterindications – that is, an instance of default reasoning.

And just this is how things stand in general. Induction is, in the end, not a peculiar way of quasi-probabilistic reasoning. It is instead, a matter of using plausible presumptive defaults in the course of straightforwardly deductive inference to plausible conclusions that provide answers to our questions.

Induction, so regarded, is accordingly not so much a process of *inference* as one of presumption-based *truth-estimation*. We clearly want to accomplish our explanatory gap-filling in the least risky, the minimally problematic way, as determined by plausibilistic considerations. This is illustrated by such examples as these:

- There is smoke yonder.
- Usually, where(ever) there's smoke, there's fire.
- < The present situation fits the usual run.>

∴ There is fire yonder.

or again

- Two-thirds of the items in the sample are defective.
- <The sample is representative of the whole.>

∴ Two thirds of the items in the whole population are defective.

(Here the enthymematically tacit premises needed to make the argument deductively cogent have been indicated.)

Its reliance on a presumption of typicality, normalcy, or the like means that any inductive process is inherently chancy. Induction rests on presumption-geared default reasoning and its conclusions are thus always at risk to further or better data since what looks to be typical or representative may in due course turn out not to be so.

4. Default Reasoning as Nonmonotonic

In virtue of the fact that default reasonings rest on a presumption of normality, typicality, or the like, it may well transpire that while a premise does indeed plausibly imply a certain conclusion, the *conjunction* of this premise with some further propositions may fail to do so. Such implications are called nonmonotonic because while "If p then q" obtains, nevertheless, it can happen that q sometimes fails to obtain in certain circumstances where p indeed holds, so that:

$$p \Rightarrow q \text{ need not yield } (p \,\&\, r) \Rightarrow q.$$

Additional information can destabilize default implications.[4]

Clearly, the monotonicity-characterizing principle,

$$\text{Whenever } p \vdash q, \text{ then } (p \,\&\, r) \vdash q,$$

works in deductive contexts, there being no way here for $p \,\&\, r$ to be true without p being so. But this will no longer be so when we replace the deductive $\vdash$ by the deductive $\Vdash$. For the reliance of default reasoning on a presumption of normality, typicality, or the like means that throughout this domain added information can undo earlier contentions.

Thus consider the claim:

If you are in America, then you might be in New York.

This is, of course, perfectly correct. But it will not do to "strengthen" the antecedent this way:

If you are in America and you are in Texas, then you might be in New York.

The conclusions we arrive at with nonmonotonic implication relations are no more than presumption. For in making the inference we have

---

4 On this sort of reasoning see Gerhard Brews, *Nonmonotonic Reasoning: Logical Foundations of Common Sense* (Cambridge: Cambridge University Press, 1991). See also John McCarthy, "Circumscription – a Form of Non-monotonic Reasoning," *Artificial Intelligence*, 13 (1980): 27–30; D. McDermott and J. Doyle, "Non-Monotonic Logic," *Artificial Intelligence*, 13 (1980): 41–72; and Raymond Reiter, "Nonmonotonic Reasoning," *Annual Review of Cognitive Science*, 2 (1987): 147–86.

to presume that the situation is not one in which some yet unseen conclusion-averting circumstance comes into operation.

This state of affairs also means that with nonmonotonic implications *modus ponenes* fails: the combination of p and $p \Rightarrow q$ need not *demonstrate* that q obtains, but may do no more than to establish a *presumption* to that effect.[5]

Nonmonotonicity is thus a standard feature of default inference, as is illustrated by contrasting the following two statements:

If I had put sugar in the tea, it would have tasted fine.
If I had put sugar and cayenne pepper in the tea, it would have tasted fine.

Or again, contrast these:

If you greet him, he will answer politely.
If you greet him with an insult, he will answer politely.

After all, that first implication effectively (but tacitly) comes to this:

If you greet him *in the usual and ordinary way*, he will answer politely,

and the antecedent of the second implication violates that initial condition.

With default inferences we thus have to do with what is – from the standpoint of standard logic, a decidedly questionable mode of reasoning. For in standard logic no qualification additional to the antecedent as such can ever abrogate whatever a valid monotonic implication implies: here the antecedent will, in and of itself, suffice to guarantee the consequent. But whenever that "inevitably (invariably, unavoidably, etc.)" inclusive implication of standardly valid implication becomes weakened to "generally, usually, probably, possibly, etc.)," the monotonicity that is requisite for authentic implication is lost. To obtain a conclusion we must now suppose that nothing untoward is hidden from our sight – that nothing unmentioned intervenes. And this always brings the factor of presumption upon the scene.

---

[5] On nonmonotonic inference see the reference cited in note 1 this chapter. Moreover, the vast literature on artificial intelligence also affords a good deal of relevant material.

5. Some Comforting Considerations

But what if those normality presumptions should prove unjustified? How are we to approach conclusions arrived at by reasoning that what we see is potentially misleading? The short answer is: Cautiously! But a somewhat more informative response lies in the important prospect of *blurring* that conclusion – making it less specified and detailed. As stated at the outset, default reasoning calls for the possibility of resort to a fall-back position. And in managing our cognitive risks we can always fall back upon *vagueness* and its inherent qualifications.

With default reasoning in general and induction in particular we run the risk that our conclusions may go awry thanks to our reliance on (generally tacit) suppositions of normality or typicality that may fail in the circumstances at hand. However, to offset the risk error here we can resort to decreasing definiteness for the sake of increasing security. Thus instead of reasoning

- q is highly likely wherever p.
- In the present case p obtains.
- The present case looks to be a typical, majority-conforming one.
- \<Looks are not deceiving here.\>
- ∴   In the present case q obtains.

we would instead reason to

- In the present case q probably obtains.

By weakening that conclusion appropriately, we take a sensible step in the direction of safety. But of course likelihoods do not answer yes/no questions, and where such questions confront us we have little choice but (circumstances permitting) to chance the risks of the presumption of typicality/normality that characterize default reasoning.

Some basic facts of epistemic life come into operation here. After all, a fundamental feature of inquiry is represented by the following observation:

THESIS 1: *Insofar as our thinking is vague, truth is accessible even in the face of error.*

Thus if it is a vaguer expression of the content of B, then some of the ways for B to be false will not falsify A (but not vice versa).

Consider the situation in which you correctly accept *P*-or-*Q*. But – so let it be supposed – the truth of this disjunction roots entirely in that of *P* while *Q* is quite false. However, you accept *P*-or-*Q* only because you are convinced of the truth of *Q*; it so happens that *P* is something you actually disbelieve. Yet despite your error, your belief is entirely true.[6] Consider a concrete instance. You believe that Mr. Kim Ho is Korean because you believe him to be a North Korean. However he is, in fact a South Korean, something you would flatly reject. Nevertheless your belief that he is Korean is unquestionably correct. Thanks to the indefiniteness of that disjunctive belief at issue, the error in which you are involved, although real, is not so grave as to destabilize the truth of your belief.

This example illustrates a more far-reaching point.

THESIS 2: *There is, in general, an inverse relationship between the precision or definiteness of a judgment and its security: detail and probability stand in a complementarily competing relationship.*

It is a basic principle of epistemology that increased confidence in the correctness of our estimates can always be purchased at the price of decreased accuracy. We *estimate* the height of the tree at around 25 feet. We are *quite sure* that the tree is 25 ± 5 feet. We are *virtually certain* that its height is 25 ± 10 feet. But we are *completely and absolutely sure* that its height is between 1 inch and 100 yards. Of this we are completely sure, in the sense that we deem it absolutely certain, secure beyond the shadow of a doubt, as certain as we can be of anything in the world, so sure that we would be willing to stake our life on it, and the like. With any sort of estimate, there is always a characteristic trade-off relationship between the evidential *security* of the estimate on the one hand (as determinable on the basis of its probability or degree of acceptability), and the informative *definiteness* (exactness, detail, precision, etc.) of its asserted content on the other. Vaguer and looser statements are for that very reason more secure because they embody larger margins of error. This relationship between security and definiteness is graphically characterized by a curve of the general

---

[6] Examples of this sort indicate why philosophers are unwilling to identify *knowledge* with *true belief*, even when this is justified.

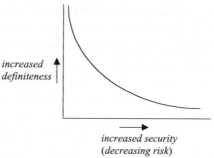

increased
definiteness

increased security
(*decreasing risk*)

DISPLAY 6.1. The security/definiteness relationship. *Note:* The overall quality of the information provided by a claim hinges on combining its security with its definiteness. Given suitable ways of measuring security (s) and definiteness (d) the curve at issue can be supposed to be an equilateral hyperbola obtained with $s \times d$ as constant.

form of an equilateral hyperbola. (See Display 6.1) and this sort of relationship holds just as well for our *truth* estimates as of others.

This state of affairs has far-reaching consequences. It means, in particular, that no highly secure statement about objective reality can say exactly and in complete detail how matters stand. To capture the truth of things by means of language we must proceed by way of "warranted approximation." In general we can be sure of how things "usually" are and how they "roughly" are, but not how they always and exactly are. And this impels our reasoning in the direction of presuppositions of normalcy, typicality, and the like, which are characteristic of default argumentation.

But be this as it may, the present considerations indicate that plausible inference affords a paradigm instance of default reasoning, which itself emerges in their light as an exercise in standard deductive inference subject to a recourse to the potentially defeasible presumption of typicality.

Yet how is it possible for the presumption-based acceptance of a potentially defeasible thesis to qualify as rationally appropriate? The answer, as noted earlier, lies in the general principle of risk management. For what is at issue with presumption is at bottom not an endorsement of a general truth but the implementation of a principle, and thus in effect, the adoption of a policy. And rationality here – as elsewhere in matters of practical procedure – pivots on the principle of a favorable balance of potential benefit over potential loss. In many situations default reasoning affords the best available pathway to our ultimately very practical requirement for information – for answering in a cogent and circumstantially responsible way a question that we need to resolve.

7

Presumption and Trust

1. The Advantages of Cooperation

In everyday life we ordinarily presume in the absence of indications to the contrary that what people tell us is what they take to be true. Analogously, we trust in the information proffered in dictionaries, encyclopedias, and reference works and rely on the counsel of doctors and other technical experts. And, reaching well beyond such authoritative sources we operate on the idea that people so function that the presumptions of Display 7.1 are plausible. What is the rationale that validates this optimistic policy of presumption based on trust?

Ultimately it is because we believe that a rational society organizes itself to motivate people strongly in this direction. For it is all too clear that substantial advantages accrue to a community and its members through creating a system that promotes trust by providing an inducement for people to be candid and honest while at the same time imposing strong sanctions against cheating, falsification, carelessness, dishonesty, and the like.

Of course all of those trustful presumptions are defeasible. We know full well that such corresponding generalizations as "People always mean what they say" simply don't hold. But the policy that underwrites those presumptions nevertheless makes good sense on the basis of the systemic considerations canvassed in the preceding chapter. And we can easily see that a contrary practice – one that takes a skeptical or agnostic stance toward the declarations of

- To trust that people mean what they say.
- To trust that people will keep their word and honor their promises; that they will not lie and cheat.
- To trust that people will meet their obligations.
- To trust that people can be prevailed on to act for the common good.

DISPLAY 7.1. Presumptions of social interaction

others – would be disastrous. For if, instead of treating those with whom one communicates on the basis of "innocent until proven guilty," one were to treat them on the lines of "not trustworthy until proven otherwise," this procedure would clearly prove vastly less economic. We would now have to resort to endless checks and tests before we could achieve any informative benefits from the communicative contributions of others.

Then too there is also the reverse side to the coin. As already stressed in the preceding chapter, if we do not concede *some* credit to the declarations of others, then we lose any and all chance to derive informative profit from them, thus denying ourselves the benefit of a potentially useful resource. Experience would soon teach us that even where strangers outside the family circle are concerned, the benefits of conceding trust, reliance, and credibility generally overbalance the risks involved. After all, even people who do not much care to cooperate and collaborate with others are well advised in terms of their own interests to suppress this inclination.

And so we proceed in these matters in the two-stage manner characteristic of presumption at large: we are trustful in the first instance because we have no more promising alternative, and then ultimately we trust when there is a supportive track record. At the start, however, we take something of a leap in the dark.

This point is brought home by considering the matter from the perspective of Display 7.2.

By hypothesis, each of the parties involved here prioritizes the situation when they are trusted by the other while they themselves need not reciprocate. And each sees as the worst case a situation when they trust without being trusted. Each, however, is willing to trust to avert being mistrusted themselves. Relative to these suppositions, we

I Trust You	You Trust Me	My Preference Ranking	Your Preference Ranking
+	+	2	2
+	−	4	1
−	+	1	4

DISPLAY 7.2. A preferential overview of trust situations

arrive at the overall situation of the interaction matrix exhibited in Display 7.2.[1] (Here the entry 2/2 – for example – indicates that in this case the outcome ranks 2 for me and 2 for you.) It is clear that mutual trust is the best available option – the only plausible way to avert the communally unhappy result 3/3. In this sort of situation, cooperative behavior is obviously the best policy. We are, after all, going to end up acting alike since, owing to the symmetry of the situation, whatever constitutes a good reason for you to act in a certain way does so for me as well. (This is a salient aspect of what might be called the Uniformizing Impartiality of Reason.)

"Why should such trust in the beliefs of people-in-general carry any weight with me?" The flippant reply here is "What is so special about me that what is accepted by them should not be acceptable to me?" But the deeper and better reason is that it is both proper and expedient that I should trust them. No other single consideration speaks as strongly for accepting the need for and desirability of trust in others in the management of our interpersonal affairs – cognitive and practical alike. And this approach has special cogency in these communicative matters where – unlike situations of outright competitive rivalry – there are commonalities of interest absent in other contexts of game-theory analysis where conflicts of interest play a more prominent role.

---

[1] The situation is one of the sort called prisoner's dilemma by game theorists. For a good account, see Morton D. Davis, *Game Theory* (New York: Basic Books, 1970), pp. 92–103. See also A. Rappoport and A. M. Chammah, *Prisoner's Dilemma: A Study in Conflict and Cooperation* (Ann Arbor: University of Michigan Press, 1965); Anatol Rappoport, "Escape from Paradox," *American Scientist*, 217 (1967): 50–56; and Richmond Campbell and Lanning Sowden (eds.), *Paradoxes of Rationality and Cooperation* (Vancouver: University of British Columbia Press, 1985).

The advantage of mutual trust is particularly clear in regard to cognitive matters. It is easy to see that a skeptical presumption – one that rejects trust and maintains a distrustful stance toward the declarations of others – would present great difficulties in interpersonal communication. Suppose that, instead of treating others as *innocent until proven guilty*, one were to treat them as *not trustworthy until proven otherwise*. It is clear that such a procedure would be vastly less economic. For we would now have to go to all sorts of lengths in independent verifications. The problems here are so formidable that we would obtain little informative benefit from the communications of others. When others tend to respond in kind to one's cooperativeness or uncooperativeness, then no matter how small one deems the chances of their cooperation in the present case, one is nevertheless well advised to act cooperatively.

From the angle of rational economy in cognitive matters there are, accordingly, substantial advantages to collaboration in inquiry, particularly in scientific contexts. For the individual inquirer, it decreases the chances of coming up completely empty-handed (though at the price of having to share the credit of discovery). For the community, it augurs a more rational division of labor through greater efficiency by reducing the duplication of effort. As long as interagents inductively react to cooperation, responding to its evident advantages with some tendency to reciprocation in future situations, cooperative behavior will yield long-run benefits. The presumption of trustworthiness is part and parcel of this situation.

2. Building up Trust: An Economic Approach

The process through which mutual trust is built up in matters of information development and management among people is best understood by means of an economic analogy that trades on the dual meaning of the idea of credit. We proceed in cognitive matters in much the same way that banks proceed in financial matters. We extend credit to others, doing so at first to only a relatively modest extent. But beyond this initial and presumptive benefit of doubt, trust has to be earned. When and if people comport themselves in a manner that shows that this credit was well deserved and warranted, we proceed to give them more credit and extend their credit limit. By responding to trust in a responsible way, one improves one's credit rating in cognitive contexts much as in financial contexts. The same sort of mechanism is at work in both cases: recognition of creditworthiness engenders a reputation on which further credit can be based; earned credit is like money in the bank, well worth the measures needed for its maintenance and for preserving the good name that is now at stake.

And this situation obtains not just in the management of information in natural science but in many other settings as well, preeminently including the information we use in everyday-life situations. For example, we constantly rely upon experts in a plethora of circumstances, continually placing reliance on doctors, lawyers, architects, and other professionals. They too must so perform as to establish credit, not just as individuals but, no less crucially, for their profession as a whole.[2]

Much the same holds for other sources of information. The example of our senses is a particularly striking case in point. Consider the contrast between our reaction to the data obtained in sight and dreams. Dreams, too, are impressive and seemingly significant data. Why then do we accept sight as a reliable cognitive source but not dreams – as people were unquestionably at first minded to do? Surely not because of any such substantive advantages as vividness, expressiveness, or memorability. The predisposition to an interest in dreams is clearly attested by their prominence in myth and literature. Our confident reliance on sight is not a consequence of its intrinsic preferability but is preeminently a result of its success in building up credit in just the way we have been considering. We no longer base our judgments about reality on dreams simply because doing so does not pay.

Trust is, of course, something that we can have not only in people but in cognitive sources at large. For a not dissimilar story holds for our information-generating technology – for telescopes, microscopes, computing machinery, and so on. We initially extend some credit because we simply must, since such instruments are our only means for

[2] Compare H. M. Vollmer and D. L. Mills (eds.), *Professionalization* (Englewood Cliffs: Prentice Hall, 1966). This credit, once earned, is generally safeguarded and maintained by institutional means: licensing procedures, training qualifications, professional societies, codes of professional practice, and the like.

a close look at the moon, at microbes, and so on. But subsequently we increase their credit limit (after beginning with blind trust) because we eventually learn, with the wisdom of hindsight, that it was quite appropriate for us to proceed in this way in the first place. As we proceed, the course of experience indicates, retrospectively as it were, that we were justified in deeming them creditworthy. In this regard the trustworthiness of people and the reliability of instrumental resources are closely analogous.

Such presumptions of reliability as that represented by the presumption of the trustworthiness of others illustrates this economic/pragmatic line of validation. Where would we be in respect to the communicative project without the presumption of reliability? Contrast two hypothetical communities: the Trusters and the Distrusters. The Trusters operate on the principle: "Be candid yourself and also accept what other people say as truthful" – at any rate in the absence of collaboration, coordination, and indeed even of effective communication. "The Distrusters operate on the principle: "Be deceitful yourself. And look on the assertions of others in the same light – as ventures in deception and deceit. Even when ostensibly being truthful, they are only trying to lure you into a false sense of security." It is clear at once that the policy of the Distrusters is totally destructive of any prospect of communication. If the accession of information for the enhancement of our knowledge through communication and exchange is the aim of the enterprise, the process of distrust is totally counterproductive. In intellectual as in financial commerce, trust is essential to the maintenance of communally beneficial institutions.

3. The Rationale of Epistemic Trust

Our standard cognitive practices incorporate a host of fundamental presumptions of initial credibility, in the absence of concrete evidence to the contrary. This leads to the sorts of rules of presumption as are listed in Display 7.3, already familiar from the prior discussion. And it deserves stress that all of these are – in effect – based on trust, in our sources of information: our senses, our informants, our methods, and the like. Our cognitive presumptions are, throughout, presumptions of trustworthiness.

- To believe the evidence of your own senses.
- To accept at face value the declarations of other people.
- To accept the determinacy of such standard "sources" of information as the senses and memory.
- To accept the declarations of recognized experts and authorities within the area of their expertise.
- To accept the reliability of the standardly employed cognitive aids and instruments (telescopes, calculating machines, reference works, logarithmic tables, etc.).
- To accept those answers to your questions for which the available evidence speaks most strongly.

DISPLAY 7.3. Presumptions of cognitive trust

Of course here too we know full well that various highly convenient generalizations regarding knowledge production are simply false:

- What seems to be, is.
- What people say is true.
- The simplest patterns that fit the data are actually correct.
- The most adequate currently available theory will work out.

We recognize that such contentions do not hold, however nice it would be if they did. Nevertheless, we are inclined – and well advised – to accept the theses at issue as principles of presumption. We follow the metarule: in the absence of concrete indications to the contrary, proceed as though such principles were true. Such principles of presumption characterize the way in which rational agents transact their cognitive business. Yet we adopt such practices not because we can somehow establish their validity, but because the cost-benefit advantage of adopting them is so substantial. The justification of trust in our senses, in our fellow inquirers, and in our cognitive mechanisms ultimately rests on considerations of economic rationality. And this sort of situation prevails in many other contexts. For example, the rationale of cultivating reputations for ability, as well as those for reliability, lies in the cost effectiveness of this resource in contexts of hiring, allocating one's reading time, and so on.[3]

---

[3] On this matter, see Thomas Sowell, *Knowledge and Decisions* (New York: Basic Books, 1980), especially the discussion of "Informal Relationships" on pp. 23–30.

The justification of those standard cognitive presumptions is not the factual one of the substantive generalization: "In proceeding in this way, you will come at correct information and will not fall into error." Rather, it is the methodological justification: "In proceeding in this way, you will efficiently foster the interests of the cognitive enterprise; the gains and benefits will, on the whole, outweigh the losses and costs." For it is clear that all such cognitive practices have a fundamentally economic validation. They are all cost effective within the setting of the project of inquiry to which we stand committed by our place in the world's scheme of things. They are characteristics of the most economical (and convenient) way for us to secure the data needed to resolve our cognitive problems – to secure answers to our questions about the world we live in. Accordingly, we can make ready sense of the established rules of information development and management on grounds of rational economy: they prevail because they offer what is, to all appearances, a very cost-effective option in comparison with the available alternatives.

To be sure, the risk of deception and error is present throughout our inquiries: our cognitive instruments, like all other instruments, are never failproof. Still, a general policy of judicious trust is eminently cost effective. In inquiring, we cannot investigate everything; we have to start somewhere and invest credence in something. But our trust need not be blind. Initially bestowed on a basis of mere hunch or inclination, it can eventually be tested, and can come to be justified with the wisdom of hindsight via a process of testing that can in due course provide the comforting reassurance of retrospective validation.

And this state of affairs conveys an instructive lesson. A principle of presumption represents an epistemic policy. And such policies admit of two sorts of justification: (1) the provision of a rationale based on general principles, and (2) the substantiation of a track record of effective performance. And in the case of the presumptions of reliability that are encompassed in our general policy of trust, such a validation is forthcoming on both scores.[4]

---

[4] Further considerations relevant to this chapter's themes can be found in Rescher, *Cognitive Economy* (Pittsburgh: University of Pittsburgh Press, 1989).

It is sometimes said that an epistemology based on trust is contrastive to and distinct from one that is based on evidence.[5] But this is a very questionable standpoint seeing that there is no absolute separation here. Throughout the realm of factual inquiry we can obtain evidence only on the basis of trust – in our sense, our sources, our methods. While trustworthiness is something we may initially presume, we must also eventually evidentiate it through experience. And yet experience itself is only cognitively significant where there is trust.

4. Trustful Interaction as a General Benefit

Only through cooperation based on mutual trust can we address issues whose effective resolution makes demands that are too great for any one of us alone. In the development and management of information, people are constantly impelled toward a system of collaborative social practices – an operational code of incentives and sanctions that consolidates and supports collective solidarity and mutual support. In this division of labor, trust results from what is, to all intents and purposes, a custom-consolidated compact to conduct their affairs in friendly collaboration.

The commonsensical policy of placing reliance on the opinions of people in general thus has a complex rationale. Partly it rests inductively on retrospective *evidential* grounds because with those issues that are appropriate for commonsense consensus we rarely go wrong by adopting the commonsense line. Partly it is appropriate prospectively for strictly *practical* reasons because on these questions we often need answers, and common sense provides our most hopeful recourse. Moreover, it can also be validated on *social* grounds because we humans are so constituted that we cannot live in isolation, and the creation of a trustful solidarity with our fellows is crucial to our well-being and survival. After all, the recourse to common sense is part and parcel of the basis for that confraternity of trust whose creation and maintenance is essential to human well-being. To reject common sense is to create tears in the fabric of trust that is essential to our ongoing existence as the sorts of creatures we are.

---

5 See John Hardwig, "The Role of Trust in Knowledge," *Journal of Philosophy*, 88 (1991): 693–708.

Trust in other people whose word is their bond makes the world of commerce and finance go round, and where it is absent economic prosperity grinds to a halt. And equally in ordinary life affairs, if we were not prepared to have trust in the judgments and opinions of others – at least in matters of ordinary, everyday affairs – we humans could not achieve the sort of orientation and guidance needed for the satisfactory conduct of our own thought and action.

After all, the pursuit of information in ordinary life formations is akin to the pursuit of wealth in business transactions. The financial markets in stocks or commodities futures would self-destruct if the principle, *my word is my bond*, were abrogated, since no one would know whether a trade had actually been made. In just this way, too, the market in information would self-destruct if people's truthfulness could not be relied upon. Thus in both cases, unreliable people have to be frozen out and exiled from the community. In cognitive and economic contexts alike, the relevant community uses incentives and sanctions (artificially imposed costs and benefits) to put into place a system in which people generally act in a trusting and trustworthy way. Such a system is based on processes of reciprocity that advantage virtually everyone.

5. The Presumptive Credibility of Common Sense

We are rationally entitled to see it as a plausible presumption that the people we deal with are aware of commonsense facts – that they can be credited with a knowledge of commonsense matters. And we are also entitled to presume those commonsensical facts to be true.

But how does common sense obtain such probative authority? After all, why respect common sense? Don't we sophisticates know better than the common run of people?

The credibility of common sense is bound up with the fact that its validity prevails only in a very limited domain, based as it is on the ordinary course of the everyday life of people in general. The crux of common sense is what ordinary people ordinarily think and do in response to the functional requirements of our world setting. The issues that can be decided on commonsense considerations are neither the technical issues of science and engineering nor the highly complex issues of economics or social planning. Rather they relate to what transpires within the sphere of our workaday affairs and the "ordinary course of things" in everyday life. And precisely because common sense is based on ordinary everyday experience of people in general, the bulk of whom are bound to be ordinary everyday individuals, it represents a domain from which expertise is excluded, one in which the learned enjoy no particular advantage over the vulgar – no doubt to the consternation of the former.

It must, of course, be acknowledged that the experts will "know better" in any and all matters that actually admit of expertise. Nevertheless there remains an important distinction between expertise-admitting and expertise-resisting issues. After all, with the everyday issues of everyday life where common experience can settle the issues, there is no expertise; common sense is our best resource here and for that very reason deserves to be heeded. (That itself is just common sense.) What "knowledgeable people" know better than the rest of us is not, surely, the plain-as-your-nose facts of everyday life but rather information about technical issues. But these technical matters do not – by definition – belong to the realm of common sense.

Commonsense beliefs encompass only the obvious (truistic) convictions of the ordinary resources of ordinary people about everyday matters of observation, self-awareness, reasoning, and common experience. To say of some contention that it is "only common sense" is to say that even "the man in the street" would and should regard it as an incontestable fact that is virtually self-evident. Questioning this sort of thing would mark one as a fool or a madman in the sight of ordinary people. There will indeed be issues with respect to which scientific sophistication can unravel the connections of common sense. But they are bound to be few and far between. In this regard common sense is like Otto Neuarth's sailing ship under repair in transit at sea. On occasion a rotten plank can be replaced here and there. But if one tries to do too much, or if one addresses one's efforts to the key components, the entire ship will quickly be lost.

However, while common sense is a sound and reliable guide, this is so only in the realm of everyday issues. Common sense does not resolve conundrums – it does no more (but also no less!) than to afford straightforward answers to commonplace issues. For as Jules Lachelier sensibly observed: "since man is [on balance] a reasonable being, the odds are that that which people in general think (at any rate in those matters that affect people in general) will not be unreasonable."[6]

Common sense also has an evolutionary aspect. On evolutionary principles of *natural* selection, the salient features that define a type of organism – a biological species – are the product of a process of natural selection subject to the reproductive nontransmission of the "unfit" – those (physically) unsuited to survive in the prevailing environmental condition. On evolutionary principles of *cultural* selection, by contrast, various cognitive instrumentalities are the product of a process of rational elimination, the cultural nontransmission of the "unfit" instrumentalities that do not effectively serve their intended functions. On this basis, "commonsense beliefs" are not biologically imprinted on the physical/biological constitution of the human mind but are culturally imprinted on the intellectual/cognitive constitution of a human culture. They reflect the thought-stance of people in general, yet not on the basis of biophysical considerations but rather on the basis of culturocognitive considerations. They are the fruits of experience – the collective experience of people on a large scale and over a long time, having prevailed in the struggle for cultural survival through providing information that meets the needs of the group.

To be sure, such fundamental commonsense convictions – as, for example, our belief in the causal efficacy of physical occurrences – are not (as with Thomas Reid) the products of certain innate principles of human nature rooted in human biology. Rather, they issue from principles rooted in human culture by means of rational selection. From the standpoint of the species, commonsense principles are not biologically imprinted universals but a culturally evolved commonality grounded in the collective experience with the truths of common sense reflective of the structure of human experience. And while even communal experience may not be an infallible and failproof resource, it is one that will (and given its rooting in a vastly extensive body of experience must) yield trustworthy results in the vast preponderance of cases relating to matters of everyday affairs.

[6] J. Lachelier in André Lalande, *Vocabulaire de la philosophie,* 9th ed. (Paris: Presses Universitaires de France, 1962), p. 971.

6. The Matter of Risk

Admittedly, trust does not have it all its own way. Be it in practical or cognitive matters, trust can go awry. In particular, the risk of deception and error is present throughout our inquiries. All of our cognitive instruments, like all other instruments, are far from failproof. Still, a general policy of judicious trust is eminently cost effective. In inquiring, we cannot investigate everything; we have to start somewhere and invest credence in something. But our trust need not be blind. Initially bestowed on a mere hunch or inclination, it can eventually be tested and can come to be justified with the wisdom of hindsight. And this process of testing can in due course put the comforting reassurance of retrospective validation at our disposal. A general policy of judicious trust is eminently cost effective in yielding good results in matters of cognition. After all, we cannot pursue the cognitive project – the quest for information about the world – without granting certain initial presumptions: they represent Kant-reminiscent "conditions under which alone" the securing of answers to questions about the world is even *possible*.

In trusting the senses, in relying on other people, *and even in being rational*, we always run a risk. Whenever in life we place our faith in something, we run a risk of being let down and disappointed. Nevertheless, it seems perfectly reasonable to bet on the general trustworthiness of the senses, the general reliability of our fellow men, and the general utility of reason. In such matters, no absolute guarantees can be had. But one may as well venture, for if venturing fails, the cause is lost anyhow – we have no more promising alternative to turn to. There is little choice about the matter: it is a case of "this or nothing." If we want answers to factual questions, we have no real alternative but to trust in the cognitively cooperative disposition of the natural order of things.

To be sure, it is not possible to preestablish the appropriateness of this trust by somehow demonstrating, in advance of events, that it is actually warranted. Rather, its rationale is that without it we remove the basis on which alone creatures such as ourselves can confidently live a life of effective thought and action. In such cases, pragmatic rationality urges us to gamble on trust in reason, not because it cannot fail us, but because in so doing we lose little and gain much.

With trust, matters can of course turn out badly. In being trustful, we take our chances (though of course initially in a cautious way). But one must always look to the other side of the coin as well. A play-safe policy of total security calls for not accepting anything, not trusting anyone. But then we are left altogether empty-handed. The quest for absolute security exacts a terrible price in terms of missed opportunities, forgone benefits, and lost chances. What recommends those inherently risky cognitive policies of credit extension and initial trust to us is not that they offer risk-free sure bets but that, relative to the alternatives, they offer a better balance of potential benefits over potential costs. It is the basically *economic* rationality of our cognitive policies of presumption that is their ultimate surety and warrant.

And so, when its cognitive needs and wants are strong enough, any group of mutually collaborating, rational, dedicated inquirers will in the end become a *community* of sorts, bound together by a shared practice of trust and cooperation, simply under the pressure of its evident advantage in the quest for knowledge.[7] For the policy at issue is one that pays. After all, only through cooperation based on mutual trust can we address issues whose effective resolution makes demands that are too great for any one of us alone. In the development and management of information, people are constantly impelled toward a system of collaborative social practices – an operational code of incentives and sanctions that consolidates and supports collective solidarity and mutual support. In this division of labor, trust results from what is, to all intents and purposes, a custom-consolidated compact between people to conduct their affairs in friendly collaboration.

7. The Presumptive Credibility of Experts

One of the prime faci of trust lies in the areas of expertise. Expertise is a matter of acknowledging authority: it pivots on the presumption of correctness in regard to the judgments of those "experts" within the

---

[7] The literature on theoretical issues of trust and cooperation in contexts of inquiry is virtually nonexistent. However, in regard to morality in general, this is not so. See, for example, Robert Axelrod, *The Evolution of Cooperation* (New York: Basic Books, 1984); David Gauthier, *Morals by Agreement* (Oxford: Oxford University Press, 1986); Raimo Tuomela, *Cooperation* (Dordrecht: Kluwer, 2000); and Nicholas Rescher, *Fairness* (New Brunswick, N.J.: Transaction Press, 2001).

domain of their expertise. And here expertise is a matter of perception and reception – of how widely that individual's claims to credibility are acknowledged among otherwise knowledgeable people. Accordingly, reputation is the key to the acceptance of expertise.

However, two importation caveats must be made here. The first is that expertise is highly topical in nature: it does not – should not – be seen as radiating beyond a particular, well-defined range of subject matter. Any sensible recourse to experts must recognize that there are proper limits here because ample experience teaches that expertise does not carry over from one area to another.

A second critical point is that in placing reliance on expert judgment in a particular case, we do so *on our own responsibility*. A person's reputation as an expert is no more than *evidence* of this individual's reliability in the case at hand. Established expertise does indeed provide the basis for a presumption – but an ultimately defeasible presumption – of correctness in the case at hand. But this presumption is defeasible and its bearing tentative. In accepting it as valid in the particular case, we take a step for which we ourselves – and neither the expert nor the generality that acknowledges him or her as such – are ultimately responsible. The acceptance of expert advice is a very sensible step, but it is something that we do on our own responsibility and which must therefore stand subject to the relevant sorts of safeguards.

The situation of science is particularly salient in this regard. Various authors speak of "the erosion of scientific authority" in the contemporary ("postmodern") world.[8] But of course here as elsewhere authority is domain-linked. Science, after all, is not designed to tell us where to go; it is designed to tell us how to get there efficiently once we have made up our minds about this essential preliminary. When the issue is how things work in the realm of nature – the how, when, and why of the world's processes – then science is in its natural element. Tea leaf reading and Ouija boards will not avail us here; on this sort of issue we have no promising alternative but to rely on science. But of course the issues of values, ends, and goals are something else again.

---

[8] See, for example, Richard H. Gaskins, *Burdens of Proof in Modern Discourse* (New Haven: Yale University Press, 1992), pp. 106–7.

If you ask a scientific question, then postmodern or not, you had best settle for a scientific answer: if there is a better place to turn, no one has yet told us. But if the question you raise lies outside the range of scientific facticity, then it is not only petulant but foolish of you to be contemptuous of science for not providing the answer.[9]

9 In matters of practical decision, for example, science will (or should) be able to tell you all the magnitude of a risk. But whether that risk is worth running or not is an issue science does not – cannot – address.

8

Presumption and Communication

1. Communicative Presumption

In the absence of any evidence to the contrary, we proceed on the presumption that people do what they do on the basis of reasons, granting them the benefit of the doubt in point of rationality. We take the stance that there is an explanation of the basis of what they see as good reasons for proceeding as they do – that they act as they do under the impression that some good will come of it, some benefit for themselves or others. Accordingly, when asked to explain why someone did something, it suffices that we establish that this was the rationally appropriate thing for them to do – that this is what any sensible person would have done in the circumstances. We presume people act rationally. Only as a reluctant last resort do we judge that someone has proceeded on the basis of forces or motives outside the range of their rational control. Thus here, as elsewhere, a presumption of normalcy prevails. Realizing full well that people are not always rational, we find that they (fortunately) are so *generally* and *ordinarily*, and feel free to proceed on this basis. We grant people the benefit of any doubt and treat them as rational agents in the absence of convincing counterindications. The rational economy of process is clearly at work here.

Cognitive convenience tells the whole story here. A world in which we cannot communicate and collaborate with others is not a very safe world for us and our kind, so evolutionary processes dictate our impetus to increasingly complex communication and collaboration. We cannot communicate or collaborate with others in the absence of a supposition of (a fair degree of) rationality on their part. Its highly practical nature accordingly contributes importantly to account for the presumption of rationality.

Again, the application of many of the generic concepts that we use in characterizing the natural and the artificial features of the world we live in – concrete particularity, lawfulness, functionality, and normativity preeminent among them – calls for leaps beyond the information we do, or ever can, actually have in hand through the evidential instrumentalities at our disposal. But what is the rationale that authorizes their use? What justifies the fact-transcendent leaps that are involved in their employment?

The answer here is that they all rest on the practice of presumption – of taking for granted that which is not actually given in the information at our disposal. Thus consider the following course of reasoning:

> It looks like a duck.
> It quacks like a duck.
> It waddles like a duck.
>
> ---
>
> Therefore: It is a duck.

This reasoning is clearly not deductively valid. (Mechanical ducks can do all those things as well.) Nor is it enthymematically valid. To be sure, we proceed on the idea that what seems to be so actually is, but this hardly qualifies as a matter of fact. Any premises we might add that actually manage to close the deductive gap fully and completely – whatever looks, quacks, and waddles like a duck will actually *be* a duck, for example – will simply not be true. And in fact nothing that we can add by way of epistemically *available* truth will close the deductive gap.

What is at issue here is not so much an inference as a leap via presumption. Such tenability as the argument has it obtains from a certain *practical policy: as long as no counterindications come to light, to treat as a duck anything that (sufficiently) behaves like one.* And this is a *praxis* rather than a factual claim of some sort. We know full well that it is false to claim that whatever looks, quacks, and waddles like a duck will actually be a duck. But in ordinary circumstances (in the absence of visible counterindications) we feel free to implement the policy at issue with an inferential leap, not because in doing so we cannot possibly go wrong, but rather because we will generally go right.

The experience-transcending leaps inherent in our cognitive presumptions are simply part of an "inductive" process built into the use of language as our instrumentality for communicating with one another about the world we live in. The validation of these highly presumption-predicated communicative resources is ultimately pragmatic rather than logico-semantical in nature. Cognitive utility is once again the crux here.

Without reliance on linguistic presumptions – on use conditions as distinct from truth conditions – inductively grounded communication would become impracticable. In no other way can the gap between the secured warrant for our objective assertions and their assertoric content be bridged over. The authorization to proceed in the indicated way is built inductively into the very fabric of the language we employ in formulating our informative claims about the world's affairs. Inherent is the fundamental defining conventions that define and specify our employment of language.

2. Truth Conditions and Use Conditions

Communication regarding the world's facts is predicated on the policy of maintaining a proper coordination between truth conditions and use conditions – between what we actually claim and what is available in the information at our disposal in the circumstances – by means of a manifold of procedural presumptions.

The rationale of information transcending presumptions is deeply rooted in the communicative modus operandi of language. Any adequate theory of language must come to terms with the difference between semantics and pragmatics by acknowledging the crucial distinction between use conditions and truth conditions. The use conditions encompass *the user-oriented circumstances in which a sentence is appropriately and warrantedly assertable by those who employ the particular language in which it figures.* The truth conditions, by contrast, detail *the reality-oriented circumstances that must obtain for the claim that is staked to be true.* The former provide the *operational criteria* for making the assertion at issue; the latter indicate the entire range of the *objective circumstances* that must obtain for the statement to be made *correctly* (i.e., truly) – including the whole gamut of inferential consequences that must be taken to follow from its assertion.

The truth conditions look to the circumstances that have to obtain for a statement to be true – as for example, "There are no witches" coordinates with a world without witches. On this basis, any claim whatever that is logically entailed by a given contention will figure among its truth conditions. Suppose that the consequence C follows inferentially from the statement S: that S entails C. Then, of course, not-C would (by contraposition) entail that not-S, so that the obtaining of C would ipso facto be encompassed among the truth conditions of S. The truth conditions of a statement accordingly encorporate the sum total of what must be the case for that initial statement to be true.

By contrast, the use conditions of a language comprise the *authorizing criteria for making the assertions at issue* by specifying the sorts of cognitive or epistemic circumstances that qualify a statement as being made *appropriately* (i.e., warrantedly), the circumstances under which the staking of those claims by a language user are in order – including what sorts of further circumstances would abrogate such entitlements.[1] They encompass not only the evidential situation but also the general setting of the communicative circumstances in which a particular assertion is validated as appropriate within the setting of the communicative practice at issue. Accordingly, communication policy plays the pivotal role in this context. For while truth conditions deal with the conceptual facts, use conditions deal with the linguistic properties.

Use conditions look to the evidential situations in which that statement can appropriately be claimed to obtain – as is certainly the case in the present state of general knowledge about witchcraft and its ways. When I see what seems to be an apple in the grocer's bin next to

---

[1] To be sure, inferential relationships obtain either way – there are both *truth* implications and *use* implications. The latter gives rise to what H. P. Grice called conversational implicatures. See his posthumous *Studies in the Ways of Words* (Cambridge, Mass.: Harvard University Press, 1989).

a label reading "Fresh Macintoshes, 30¢ per pound," I quite appropriately take the *use* conditions for the claim "Those objects are apples" to be fully and amply satisfied. But, of course, *truth* conditions are something else again, seeing that they involve a vast deal more – to wit, that those objects have apple cores at their middle rather than sand; that they grew on apple trees rather than being synthesized in an apple-replicator; that they are not strangely deformed pears of some sort, and so on.

And, of course, what is at issue with truth conditions is something far above and beyond the vastly more modest matter of use conditions. If the circumstances are such that a proposition's *truth* conditions are not satisfied, then this proposition is false. But if the circumstances are such that a proposition's *use* conditions are not satisfied, then this proposition is not necessarily false, but its assertion is merely inappropriate or unwarranted. No secure inference about its truth can be made one way or the other. The failure here is not an error of commission but an error of omission – of not properly equipping one's claim with an appropriate grounding. When the use conditions are satisfied in the context of a speaker's claim we might well wind up saying that the speaker had spoken *falsely* but not that the speaker had spoken *inappropriately*, let alone "in reckless disregard for the truth."

It would be very mistaken to think of the conditions of use or assertability as consisting in explicitly formalized rules alone. In general, what is at issue is not, strictly speaking, a matter of *rules* at all. The use conventions at issue are not always formulated and codified; doubtless they are not fully codifiable, any more than are the rules for hitting a forehand in tennis. What is at issue is a matter of the characterizing conditions of a practice, of how-to-do-it guidelines, of the skills and tricks of the linguistic trade, of what is learned largely through observation, imitation, and habituation rather than through mastery of and adherence to explicitly specifiable rules. (There are, obviously, some things we must be able to do without using rules – following rules, for example, since otherwise we would be in the paradoxical situation of needing rules to govern the use of rules.) Language users can observe the proprieties without mastering them in a codified form.

The communicative use of presumption is no more based on learning and applying rules than is running or catching a ball.

The truth conditions of a statement are a matter of the *semantics* of a language; the use conditions are a matter of what has come to be called its *pragmatics.*[2] These use conditions are intrinsic components of the language – a part of what children learn about the use of their native tongue at mother's knee. Truth conditions do not have a monopoly on "meaning" – this concept is broad enough to encompass both sorts of conditions. After all, the use conditions and their correlative imputational ground rules are every bit as much an aspect of the meaning of our words as are the truth conditions. These two aspects of meaning (consequences via truth condition and antecedents via warranting or use conditions) stand in a symbiotic intertwining. A crucial part of learning what a word *means* is to learn how it is *used* – that is, to get a working grasp of the types of conditions and circumstances under which its use in certain ways is *appropriate.* And here it is necessary to realize that this involves an inductive component – an implicit view of "the way in which things work in the world."

But are not truth conditions the pivotally crucial thing for meaning? Surely you don't really know what a statement means if you don't know fully and exactly what follows from it. This seems altogether plausible – but only because we theorists are so deeply invested in the logical (rather than practical) sense of meaning. Semantics has dominated over pragmatics in recent language studies, but both are needed. Granted, without grasping the truth conditions of a statement we would not know exactly what it claims. But, equally important, without access to its use conditions, we would not know when it is actually in order to stake a claim. Neither aspect is dispensable; they are conjointly requisite.

The critical fact is that meaning is a comprehensive concept that embraces both semantic and pragmatic issues. To gain an adequate grasp of a language we must learn *both* what follows from its statements

---

[2] On pragmatics, see S. Levinson, *Pragmatics* (Cambridge: Cambridge University Press, 1983), and Levinson, *Presumptive Meanings* (Cambridge, Mass.: MIT Press, 2002); G. Gazdar, *Pragmatics, Implications, Presupposition, and Logical Form* (New York: Academic Press, 1979) and G. Ward and L. Harn (eds.), *Handbook of Pragmatics* (Oxford: Blackwell, 2003).

and what authorizes them – what conditions allow us to take them to be in order. Any exclusivistic doctrine along the lines of meaning is use, or meaning is a matter of truth conditions, is one-sided, dogmatic, *and* inappropriate in its claim to exclusiveness.

Use conditions accordingly reflect a practical policy of presumption. The legitimation of the practical policy at work here is ultimately the matter of convenience. As is generally the case with practical policies, the process is at bottom a matter of cost-benefit calculations. Language simply could not develop as an effective instrument of communication (information transmission) if the use-to-truth transition were not generally feasible.[3]

This idea of such presumptive "taking" is a crucial aspect of our language-deploying discursive practice. For one thing it is the pivot point for the objectivity of language use – for its intensionality (with an S) in point of application to real-world objects. The actual starting point may be no more than "I take myself to be seeing an apple." But we readily go beyond this idea to "I take it to be an apple that I see," and then move beyond this thought to *claim*: "I see an apple." And these transitions – this move from experiential subjectivity to our objective and factual claims – find their warrant in the established principles and practices of language use, that is, in these use rules of language. It is not that that apple is somehow *given* to us in "brute experience." (Wilfrid Sellars's critique of "The Myth of the Given" was perfectly in order.) But beyond that mythological *given* there lies the reality of what is putatively *taken* by us: the reality of what we take to be so subject to the established use rules of linguistic policy and praxis. The justification of those use rules certainly does not lie in observational evidentiation with respect to the given, seeing that we simply cannot deploy any experience-transcending "observation" to reach behind experience to the subexperiential reality behind what we had experienced. Rather than being evidential in *this* sort of way, the justification of those use rules is pragmatic. It lies in considerations of utility – in the effectiveness with which they enable us to realize the relevant purposes of the context, which in this linguistic case comes to

---

[3] Some other issues relevant to the present deliberations are discussed in Rescher, *The Primacy of Practice* (Oxford: Basil Blackwell, 1973), as well as chapter 1 (Meaning and Assertability) of *Empirical Inquiry* (Totowa, N.J.: Rowman and Littlefield, 1982).

the guidance of our own actions and the concerting of those actions through communication with others.

3. Communication and the Presumption of Normalcy

Once a practice of presumption is in place within a community, a communicator in its orbit will be presumed not only to be aware of it but to honor it as well. In particular, he will be presumed to authorize its application with respect to his own discourse. His statements will thus in effect carry with them an "inference license" that authorizes their recipients to accept all of those consequences, presuppositions, and connectivities that fall within the established presumption range of his statements.

It must be stressed, however, that talk of "inference" here is metaphysical. Strictly speaking, what is at issue is by no means an "inference" – it is less a matter of *dedication* than one of *interpretation*. Consider an example. I tell you that I have just come from a meeting downtown with your uncle and that he sends you his regards. You conclude on this basis that he has not turned green and sprouted a second head. This "conclusion" does not in any sense follow from what I said; it simply roots in the circumstance that I did not say something else. It is a standard aspect of communicative practice not to skip over important issues, and in particular not to let big deviations from the usual course of things to pass by unremarked in a relevant observation. That "conclusion" is not something that is *given* by what I said; it is *taken* by you from the contextual consideration of what I did not say. And this taking is not arbitrary and unwarranted; it is authorized by the ground rules of communicative practice to which we subscribe throughout our linguistic interactions. In saying what I do, I effectively warrant you in arriving at that "conclusion," and to do so not by a *valid deduction* but by an *authorized presumption*.

In matters of securing information, we simply cannot start at square one and do everything by ourselves. We must – and do – proceed in the setting of a larger community that extends across the reaches of time (via its cultural traditions) and space (via its social organization). This requires communication, coordination, and collaboration. And so even as the pursuit of objectivity is aided by an agent's recourse to the resources of the envisioning community, so conversely, is objectivity an indispensable instrumentality for the creation and maintenance of an intercommunicative community as such. There can be no community where people do not understand one another, and it is the endeavor to proceed as any rational person would in my place that renders my proceedings efficiently intelligible to others. (Here too the uniformizing principle of the Impartiality of Reason is at work.)

In extracting information from the declarations of others we do – and must – rely on a whole host of working assumptions and presumptions. The pivotal factor here lies in the circumstance that verbal communication in informative contexts is governed by such conventions as these:

- Speakers and writers purport their contentions to present the truth as they believe them to be. (This is why saying "The cat is on the mat and I don't believe it" is paradoxical.)
- Speakers and writers purport their contention to be formulated in a way that is accurate and not misleading.

Such conventions are not *hypotheses* regarding the actual modus operandi of speakers. They are something quite different, namely, *imputations* that we ourselves make in the interests of communicative efficacy. For it is through imputing to our interlocutors an intention to convey relevant information (and the like) that we are best able to draw informative benefit from our communicative interactions.

Accordingly, such conventions have a well-based rationale in considerations of communicative efficiency and effectiveness, since in their absence communication would become at most impossible and at best vastly more cumbersome, Byzantine, and problematic. The coordination of common sense inherent in the standard communicative presumptions is an integral and indispensable component of this enterprise.

A significant feature of normal communication is that it follows a policy of not saying what does not really need to be said. That presumption of normalcy – that the relevant circumstances and conditions stand in their prosaically normal and natural condition unless otherwise indicated – is a crucial factor in communicative economy – an important communicative ground rule that authorizes all sorts of inferences *ex silentio*. This enables us to convey without explicit mention the fact of "business as usual" in the vast majority of circumstances where this is the case. In the absence of such a presumption it would become next to impossible to communicate efficiently. If I merely say "She gave birth to a child" you are on safe ground in concluding that it was a normal child and not, say, a pair of Siamese twins. To be sure, this conclusion "follows" not so much from what I said as from what I did not say. For either of these possible eventuations would have been so newsworthy, so contextually significant that there is every expectation that the speaker would have mentioned it had it been the case.

Again, when we are discussing someone – say, someone I know whom you are about to meet at a party – we operate with the tacit convention that I will tell you the relevantly pertinent facts, and that in those respects that I pass over, the situation is ordinary and normal. If the person is a male who has lost a hand in battle, I would certainly be expected to mention that. But I need not trouble to tell you that the individual is made of flesh and bones. There is an operative presumption of normalcy in unmentioned respects that is an essential part of the rational economy of the process.

It is part of common sense that we impute to ourselves and credit to others that in offering and extracting information in communicative contexts people will make those presumptions that allow our communicative business to be transacted smoothly and efficiently.

Some of the key presumptions of communication are reviewed in Display 8.1.[4] The presumption of relevance has special interest. If we are discussing the depressed state of the construction industry in town and you mention that Brown's Lumber Yard closed for business last month, I would feel entitled to conclude that this occurred because business was poor. If on the next day I learned that the place had burned down, I would rightly consider myself misled because that added bit of information destabilizes the otherwise perfectly plausible presumption of context-relevancy.[5]

---

4 On communicative presumptions, see H. P. Grice, *Studies in the Way of Words* (Cambridge, Mass.: Harvard University Press, 1989). And beyond this pioneering work, see also John Searle, *Speech Acts* (Cambridge: Cambridge University Press, 1969); Donald Davidson and Gilbert Harman (eds.), *The Logic of Grammar* (Encino, Calif.: Dickenson, 1975);

5 On the presumption of relevance, see David Sperbar and Deirdre Wilson, *Relevance: Communication and Cognition* (Oxford: Blackwell, 1986; 2nd ed., 1995).

- To recognize what is explicitly said as the most relevantly significant aspect of the matter.
- To accept one's interlocutor's *semantical competence* (e.g., that the person knows the meaning of the words he or she uses).
- As so, to construe what one's interlocutor says in its normal signification; to take what people say at face value.
- To accept one's interlocutor's *good faith* (e.g., that the person intends to affirm what his or her words mean).
- And so, to accept one's interlocutor's veracity; to accept as true what one's interlocutor maintains to be so.
- To accept one's interlocutor's *logical competence*; to credit the speaker with accepting the logical consequences of what he or she says.
- To credit one's interlocutors with rational cogency by construing what is said in whatever sense makes it maximally relevant to the issue under discussion.

DISPLAY 8.1. Some key communicative presumptions

There is also the closely related presumption that what is left unsaid does not abrogate or otherwise crucially alter what is naturally inferred from what is actually said. And this means that in many declarative settings silence implies *normalcy*. Suppose, for example, that Smith enters and tells us that he saw a monkey at the construction site down the street. We would of course be surprised, realizing how unusual it is for this sort of primate to be at large in the town. But if on further discussion it turned out that Smith meant a pile driver with its falling hammer (also called a "monkey") we would feel misled and deceived. We would think "If *that's* the sort of monkey he meant, he should have said so." Smith's silence about the sort of nonstandard "monkey" at issue in his statement is meaningful because it authorizes the belief that it is an ordinary and familiar sort of monkey that is at issue.

Accordingly, silence has to do important communicative work. In verbal communication we never have enough time and space at our disposal to do justice to it all: to explain every detail, and then to explain the further details relating to those explanations. And the demands of communicative efficiency and economy mean, among other things, that since there is never time (or space) to say *everything* – to make explicit in practice everything that is relevant in principle, we have to operate on the natural presumption that what we do actually say is the most important part of the matter.

And presumptions regarding silence hold not just with matters of fact but with matters of fiction as well. The story tells us that the villain ate a grape but tells us nothing further about that grape. Was it unripe or fully matured, pitted or pitless, Concord or Catawba? The story does not say. But this certainly does not mean that what the villain ate was a strangely anomalous grape – ontologically indeterminate in nature as between all of these possibilities and thus of a type we never encounter in the real world. The presumption of normalcy means that we are entitled to suppose that it was a perfectly ordinary grape – and not some biologically strange sort of grape about which our information is incomplete. Stories may be indeterminate about things, but they are not about indeterminate things.

In grounding the truth about fictional things in what the stories at issue say about them, one must be careful not to go too far. In his article on fictional objects, Terence Parsons wrote that fictional objects are that of which all *and only* the sentences of the stories are true.[6] But this is deeply problematic. The Sherlock Holmes stories certainly do *not* tell us that Sherlock Holmes's paternal grandfather was not a chimpanzee. And so if *only* the Holmes characterizing statements that are explicit in the stories are true, then this sentence would lose its claim to truth, expelling Holmes from the realm of ordinary humanity in a way that is clearly absurd. However, this situation is at once remedied by adopting the standard policy of communicative presumption that silence implies normalcy. Given that the Holmes stories are otherwise silent on the subject of grandfather Holmes, we are entitled to maintain that he, too, was an ordinary human being. For the context of telling us about things – be the setting one of real life or of fiction – the presumption is operative: if anything is out of the ordinary, the narrator would tell us about it.

Communication thus proceeds on ground rules of communicative efficiency.[7] And those presumptions governing silence and normalcy

---

[6] See Terence Parsons, "A Prolegomenon to Meinongian Semantics," *Journal of Philosophy*, 71 (1974): 551–60, and also "A Meinongian Analysis of Fictional Objects," *Grazer Philosophische Studien*, 1 (1974): 73–86.

[7] On this issue see Rescher, *Cognitive Economy* (Pittsburgh: University of Pittsburgh Press, 1989).

play a pivotal role here through underwriting such principles as "what is left out is unimportant for the issue at hand," "what is left out will not significantly alter the indications plausibly drawn from what is put in," and "what is left out would not call for a substantial revision of what has been said." Effective communication would become impracticable without presumptions that enable us to fill in the gaps between what is explicitly said.

The standard presumptions that underlie our communicative practices are emphatically *not* validatable as established facts. (For example, it is certainly *not* true – save at the level of statistical generality – that people say what they mean.) But their justification becomes straightforward on economic grounds, as practices that represent the most efficient and economical way to accomplish our communicative work.

The commitment to an objective reality that lies behind the data that people secure is indispensably demanded by any step into that domain of the publicly accessible objects that is essential to communal inquiry and interpersonal communication about a shared world. We do – and must – adopt the standard policy that prevails with respect to all communicative discourse of letting the language we use, rather than whatever specific informative aims we may actually have in mind on particular occasions, be the decisive factor with regard to the things at issue in our discourse. For if we were to set up our own conception of things as somehow definitive and decisive, we would at once erect a barrier not only to further inquiry but also – no less important – to the prospect of successful communication with one another.

Communication requires not only common *concepts* but common *topics* – shared items of discussion, a shared world of self-subsistently real objects basic to communicative experience. The factor of objectivity reflects our basic commitment of a shared world as the common property of communicators. Such a commitment involves more than merely de facto intersubjective agreement. For such agreement is a matter of a posteriori discovery, while our view of the nature of things puts "the real world" on a necessary and a priori basis. This stance roots in the fundamental convention of a socially shared insistence on communicating – the commitment to an objective world of impersonal actuality that provides the crucially requisite common focus required for any genuine communication. What links my discourse with that of my interlocutor is our common subscription to the governing presumption (a defensible presumption, to be sure) that we are both talking about the shared thing, our own possible misconceptions of it notwithstanding. This means that no matter how extensively we may change our minds about the *nature* of a thing or type of thing, we are still dealing with exactly the same thing or sort of thing. It assures reidentification across discordant theories and belief systems.

Any pretentions to the predominance, let alone the correctness of our own potentially idiosyncratic conceptions about things must be put aside in the context of communication. The fundamental intention to deal with the objective order of this "real world" is crucial. If our assertoric commitments did not transcend the information we ourselves have on hand, we would never be able to "get in touch" with others about a shared objective world. No claim is made for the *primacy* of our conceptions, or for the *correctness* of our conceptions, or even for the mere *agreement* of our conceptions with those of others. The fundamental intention to discuss "the thing itself" predominates and overrides any mere dealing with the thing as we ourselves conceive of it.

Someone might, of course, possibly object as follows:

But surely we can get by on the basis of personal conceptions alone, without invoking the notion of "a thing itself." My conception of a thing is something I can convey to you, given enough time. Cannot communication proceed by correlating and matching personal conceptions, without appeal to the intermediation of "the thing itself."

But think here of the concrete practicalities. What is "enough time"? Just when is the match "sufficient" to underwrite outright identification? But such imponderables do not and need not trouble us: our commitment to the thing itself enables us to make this identification straightaway by imputation, by fiat on the basis of modest indicators, rather than on the basis of an appeal to the inductive weight of a body of evidence that is always bound to be problematic. Communication – the conveying of information – is something that *we set out* to do, and not merely something that we ultimately accounted only retrospectively, with the wisdom of eventual hindsight.

Our very concept of a *real thing* is such that it provides a fixed point, a stable center around which communication revolves, an invariant focus of potentially diverse conceptions. What is to be determinative, decisive, definitive of the things at issue in my discourse is not my conception, or yours, or indeed anyone's conception at all. The conventionalized intention discussed means that a coordination of conceptions is not decisive for the possibility of communication. Your statements about a thing can and should convey something to me even if my conception of it is altogether different from yours. For to communicate we need not take ourselves to share views of the world, but only take the stance that we share the world being discussed. This commitment to an objective reality that underlies the data at hand is indispensably demanded by any step into the domain of the publicly accessible objects essential to communal inquiry and interpersonal communication about a shared world. And indeed, we could not establish communicative contact about a common objective item of discussion if our discourse were geared to the substance of our own idiosyncratic ideas and conceptions.

The objectifying imputation at issue here lies at the heart of our cognitive stance that we live and operate in a world of real and objective things. This commitment to the idea of a shared real world is crucial for communication. Its status is a priori: its existence is not something we learn of through experience. As Kant clearly saw, objective experience is possible only if the existence of a real, objective world is *presupposed* at the onset rather than seen as a matter of ex post facto discovery about the nature of things.

And so, what is at issue here is not a matter of *discovery*, but one of *imputation*. The element of commonality, of identity of focus is not a matter of ex post facto learning from experience, but of an a priori predetermination inherent in our approach to language use. We do not *infer* things as being real and objective from our phenomenal data, but establish our perception as authentic perception *of* genuine objects through the fact that these objects are given – or rather, *taken* – as real and objectively existing things from the first. Presumption is the key here because impersonal objectivity is not deduced but imputed. We do, no doubt, *purport* our conceptions to be objectively correct, but whether this is indeed so is something we cannot tell with unqualified assurance until "all the returns are in" – that is, never.

4. Truthful Communication as a General Benefit Enterprise

The functional rationale for the standard presumption illustrated with particular vividness is the context of communication.

Suppose I tell you, The cat is on the mat. What information do you now actually have? Is it (1) The cat *is* on the mat? Or is it (2) Rescher *thinks* (believes) that the cat is on the mat? Or is it merely (3) Rescher *says* that the cat is on the mat? In the circumstances under hypothesis, only the last item is wholly unproblematic. And it is clear that one cannot manage to get from (3) to (2) unless one adds something like (4): when Rescher says something (in a serious tone of voice) he generally believes it. Moreover, you certainly cannot get from (2) to (1) unless you credit me with veracity and trustworthiness and impute to me a penchant for truth – that is, unless you also accept (5): when Rescher believes something to be so (in such matters as cats and mats, at any rate) he is generally right.

The entire process of communication – of deriving substantive information from the declarations of others – involves trust. But what validates this? To answer this question it is best to look at the issue in economic perspective. To derive benefit from the declarations of others, we must (1) listen to them, pay heed; (2) interpret (decode) what they say; (3) extend them cognitive credit by accepting it. And none of these steps is cost free: each exacts from us an outlay of resources in time, effort, attention, and risk of error. All procedures for the acquisition of information – listening, watching, reading, and so on – involve expenditures of some sort. (No school student is ever wholly oblivious to the fact that learning can be painful.) And whether this outlay is warranted depends on the correlative advantages – preeminently including the cognitive benefits of acquired information.

A communicating community is a sort of marketplace with offerers and takers, sellers and buyers. In accepting the declarations of others at their informative face value, we extend them credit, in a sense. The prospect of informative communication is predicated on such principles as these: (1) concede a presumption of veracity to the assertions of others, at any rate until such time as they prove themselves unworthy of credit; and (2) in communicative contexts, regard others as candid, truthful, accurate, and the like until proven otherwise. The rationale of such principles of epistemic procedure is largely or wholly economic. For here, as elsewhere, it is ultimately on the basis of considerations of cost effectiveness that we decide how much credit to extend.

After all, why do we credit people with communicative capacity – with the power to provide information? Note that the purported fact – *When he utters "the cat is on the mat," he is engaged in asserting that the cat is on the mat* – represents a belief of ours, or at any rate a supposition on our part. We make this supposition initially in desperation, as it were, because it provides the only feasible way for us to derive any benefit from the content of someone's assertions, but ultimately because we eventually accumulate evidence that indicates (with the wisdom of hindsight) that this supposition was well advised (warranted).

In extracting information from the declarations of others we rely on a whole host of working assumptions: (1) People mean to say what they apparently say (what we take them to be saying). (2) People believe what they say. (3) People have good grounds for their beliefs (i.e., there are such grounds and they have cognizance of them). Essentially the same justification obtains throughout: unless we enter into such communicative presumptions, we deprive ourselves of any chance to extract information from the declarations of others. On this basis, we are rationally well advised (for example) to treat their declarations as epistemically innocent until proven otherwise, exactly because this is the most cost effective thing to do. Our communicative procedures are motivated – and justified – by the essentially profit-seeking objective of extracting the maximum benefit from our information-oriented interactions.

Communication is accordingly predicated on a policy of conceding and maintaining credibility. For communication too is a commercial system of sorts. Credit is extended, drawn upon, and enlarged. And with communicative and financial credit alike, one could not build up credit (prove oneself creditworthy) unless given some credit by somebody in the first place. For credit to be obtainable at all, there has to be an initial presumption that one is creditworthy. Clearly, such a presumption of innocent until proven guilty (i.e., fault free until shown to be otherwise) can be defeated; one can of course prove oneself to be unworthy of credit or credence. But initially the presumption must be made.

The guiding principle here is that of cost-benefit calculation. The standard presumptions that underlie our communicative practices are emphatically not validatable as established facts. (For example, it is certainly *not* true that people say what they mean, save at the level of statistical generality.) But their justification becomes straightforward on economic grounds, as practices that represent the most efficient and economical way to get the job done. For if we do not credit the declarations of others, then we lose any and all chance to derive informative profit from them, thus denying ourselves the benefit of a potentially useful resource. The course of experience would then soon teach us that the benefits of trust, of credibility concession, generally overbalance the risks involved.

Not only is maintaining credibility an asset in communication, but some degree of it is in fact a necessary condition for the viability of the whole project. The precept, *Protect your credibility; do not play fast and loose with the ground rules, but safeguard your place in the community of communicators*, is basic to the communicative enterprise.

From the sender's point of view, putting forth a message calls for the expenditure of time, effort, energy, and the like. The rational agent will incur such costs only with a view to benefits – some worth of reward (if only in the respect or gratitude of others) or reciprocity, with a view to a quid pro quo. This point is simple but of far-reaching import. Given our need for information to orient us in the world (on both pure and practical grounds), the value of creating a community of communicators is enormous. We are rationally well advised to extend ourselves to keep the channels of communication to our fellows open, and it is well worth expending much for the realization of this end.

And the same sort of story holds for the receivers' point of view as well. They too must expend resources on acquiring, processing, and storing messages. Clearly, a rational hearer would be prepared to undertake this expenditure only if there were a reasonable expectation of drawing profit from it, be it by way of information obtained or pecuniary reward – an expectation which, in general, is amply warranted. We cannot begin to make sense of what we think and say if we do not honor the conventions that define the very language in which our claims and assertions are formed.

5. Rational Economy as the Crux

The efficacy of the communicatively standard principles of presumption has other aspects as well. Why should we credit other people with communicative potential – with the capacity to provide us with information? Note that the purported fact – In uttering "the cat is on the mat" he is engaged in asserting that the cat is on the mat – represents a belief of ours, or at any rate a supposition on our part. We make such communicative suppositions initially in desperation, as it were, because this provides the only feasible way for us to derive any benefit from the content of someone's assertions, but ultimately because we eventually accumulate evidence that indicates (with the wisdom of hindsight) that this supposition was well advised (warranted), if not invariably then at least by and large. On this basis, we are rationally well advised, for example, to treat their declarations as epistemically innocent until proven otherwise, exactly because this is the most cost-effective thing to do. Our communicative procedures are motivated – and justified – by the essentially economic objective of extracting the maximum benefit from our information-oriented interactions.

The communicative policy of accepting at face value what we are told in the absence of any case-specific counterindications is in place because it is always in our interest to proceed in ways that are efficient and effective in meeting our informational requirements. If playing safe were all that mattered, we would, of course, suspend judgment indefinitely. But it is simply not in our interest to do so, since safety is not all. A policy that would deprive us of any and all communicative benefit is inherently counterproductive. In rational inquiry we seek not only to avert error but also to achieve knowledge. We adopt an epistemic policy of credence in the first instance because it is the most promising avenue toward our goals, and then persist in it because we subsequently find, not that it is unfailingly successful, but that it is highly cost effective.[8]

And not only is the maintenance of credibility an asset to communication, but some degree of it is in fact an outright necessity. The precept "Protect your credibility; do not play fast and loose with the social ground rules, but safeguard your place in the community of communicators" is basic to the entire project of communication. And so, practices that discernibly lead in this direction are for that very reason the more likely to be tried and, once tried, retained.

---

[8] Usefully relevant discussions can be found in David Lewis, *Convention: A Philosophical Study* (Cambridge, Mass.: Harvard University Press, 1969). But contrast Angus Ross, "Why Do We Believe What We are Told?" *Ratio*, 28 (1986): 69–88.

A society of intelligent agents is pretty well destined to evolve under the pressure of rational self-interest into a kind of mutual aid association whose members are engaged in a collaboration in the management of information. For, clearly, everyone benefits from a systemic *modus operandi* that maintains the best balance of costs and benefits for each of us in creating a communally usable pool of knowledge. And communication is accordingly predicated on conceding and maintaining credibility.

In the end, communication is a commercial system of sorts. Credit is extended, drawn upon, and, when all goes well, enlarged. And with communicative and financial credit alike, one could not build up credit (prove oneself creditworthy) unless given *some* credit by somebody in the first place. For credit to be obtainable at all, there has to be an initial presumption that one is creditworthy. In communicative contexts too, such a presumption of innocence until proven guilty – free of fault until shown to be otherwise – is indispensable. To be sure, such a presumption can be defeated; one can of course prove oneself to be unworthy of credit or credence. But nevertheless, the operation of those presumptions "as a rule" is critical for the viability of the entire communicative enterprise.

9

Presumption in Science and Beyond

1. Presumptions in Science

Philosophers of science often puzzle about the prominent but yet problematic role of such theoretical factors of inductive reasoning as *regularity, continuity, simplicity, uniformity, conservation*, and the like. It would clearly be problematic to regard such factors as representing fundamentally ontological facts about the world – an inclination on the part of nature itself (to put it somewhat anthropomorphically). It would, however, make perfectly good sense to view such factors as representing *principles of procedural presumption* – forming part of the regulative or methodological mechanism of our vehicles of explanation. One thereby avoids treating such features of systematicity as substantive findings about nature but rather as methodological, and procedural guideposts for our conduct of scientific inquiry – procedural principles of plausibility that constitute our evaluative standards for explanatory accounts.

In this way, a positive presumption of acceptability is taken to operate in favor of all the traditional parameters of systematization: consistency, uniformity, regularity (causality, rulishness, and lawfulness in all forms), simplicity, connectedness/coherence, unity/completeness, and the rest. These various defining facets of systematicity thus come to do double duty as elements of a criteriology for acceptability-as-true and as presumptive principles regulatively governing the conduct of inquiry. The resulting situation is set out in Display 9.1.

- To endorse as best the most strongly evidentiated theory (or explanation). And moreover,
- To accept the simpler of otherwise equally adequate theories (or explanations), so that comparatively more complex theories (or explanations) are never to be adopted where comparatively simpler ones will do. And moreover,
- The same goes for such cognate factors as uniformity, regularity, continuity, simplicity, and conservation. Moreover, it is the universal practice in scientific theory construction, when other things are anything like equal, to give preference to
- one-dimensional rather than multidimensional modes of description,
- quantitative rather than qualitative characterizations,
- lower rather than higher-order polynomials,
- linear rather than nonlinear differential equations.

DISPLAY 9.1. Some presumptions of scientific inquiry

The methodological standing of such factors as principles of epistemic presumption is reflected in the schema:

Other things being (anything like) equal, give precedence in acceptance-deliberations to those alternatives that, in the context of other actual or putative commitments, are relatively more uniform (or coherent or simple or complete, etc.) than their alternatives.

On this basis, the definitive parameters of systematicity serve as guiding principles of plausibility and presumption, transmuting them from *descriptive principles of system structure* into *procedural principles of presumption in system construction*. Accordingly, the role in scientific reasoning of factors like continuity, simplicity, uniformity, and all the other cognitive desiderata embraced within the ambit of inductive systematization, should (and can) be validated as rational from the angle of probative methodology. These factors accordingly regulate the sorts of presumptions that it is reasonable to make in the absence of any explicit indications to the contrary in scientific contexts. They represent presumptions that are "in possession of the field" as the scientist goes about the work of constructing explanatory accounts regarding the phenomena of nature.

These deliberations lead back straightaway to the analysis of inductive reasoning outlined in Chapter 6. Let us reexamine this aspect of the matter from the different vantage point now at issue.

2. Induction and Cognitive Economy: The Economic Rationale of Simplicity Preference

Induction as a key instrument of scientific reasoning is a matter of projecting our cognitive commitments just as far beyond the data as is necessary to get answers for our questions, staying as close to the data as possible while proceeding under the aegis of established principles of inductive systematization: simplicity, harmony, uniformity, and the rest. Presumption in favor of economy and simplicity are the guiding principles of inductive reasoning, whose procedure is that of the precept: "Resolve your cognitive problems in the simplest, most economical way compatible with an adequate use of the information at your disposal. Induction proceeds by way of constructing the most economical structures to house the available data comfortably." It is standard practice to discern the simplest overall pattern of regularity that can adequately accommodate our information regarding cases in hand and then project them across the entire spectrum of possibilities in order to answer our general questions. Induction is thus a process of implementing the general idea of cognitive economy by building up the simplest structure capable of resolving our cognitive problems. As a fundamentally inductive endeavor, scientific theorizing accordingly involves the search for, or the construction of, the systematically optimal theory structure capable of adequately accommodating the currently available data.

Simpler (more systematic) answers are more easily codified, taught, learned, used, investigated, and so on. In short, they are more economical to operate. In consequence, the regulative principles of convenience and economy in learning and inquiry suffice to provide a rational basis for systematicity preference. Our penchant for simplicity, uniformity, and systematicity in general is not a matter of a substantive theory regarding the nature of the world but one of search strategy – of cognitive methodology. In sum, we opt for simplicity (and systematicity in general) in inquiry because it is teleologically effective for the more cost-efficient realization of the goals of the enterprise, for the parameters of inductive systematicity – simplicity, uniformity, regularity, normality, coherence, and the rest – all represent practical principles of cognitive economy.[1] They are labor-saving devices for the avoidance of complications in the course of our endeavors to realize the objects of inquiry. The rationale of simplicity preference is thus straightforward. It lies in the single word *economy*. The simplest workable solution is that which is the easiest, most straightforward, most inexpensive one to work with. It is the very quintessence of foolishness to expend greater resources than are necessary for the achievement of our governing objectives. And by its very nature, induction affords us the most cost-effective – the economically optimal – means for accomplishing an essential cognitive task.

In all contexts, cognitive ones included, the rational agent opts for the simplest workable solution. We certainly do not do this because we know from the outset that the simple answers are bound to prove correct. Rather, we adopt the simplest viable solutions until further notice (i.e., until they may prove to be no longer viable) just exactly because they are the simplest – just because there is by hypothesis no good reason whatsoever for resorting to a more complex possibility. The rational basis for preferring inductive simplicity lies in considerations of the economic dimension of practice and procedure rather than in any factual supposition about the world's nature.

The ideas of economy and simplicity are the guiding principles of inductive reasoning. The procedure is that of the precept: "Resolve your cognitive problems in the simplest, most economical way compatible with an adequate use of the information at your disposal." Our penchant for simplicity is easy to justify on grounds of cognitive economy. If one claims a phenomenon to depend not just on certain distances and weights and sizes, but also (say) on such further factors

---

[1] Kant was the first philosopher clearly to perceive and emphasize this crucial point: "But such a principle [of systematicity] does not prescribe any law for objects; . . . it is merely a subjective law for the orderly management of the possessions of our understanding, that by the comparison of its concepts it may reduce them to the smallest possible number; it does not justify us in demanding from the objects such uniformity as will minister to the convenience and extension of our understanding; and we may not, therefore, ascribe to the [methodological or regulative] maxim [Systematize knowledge!] any objective [or descriptively constitutive] validity" (CPuR., A306 B362.). Compare also C. S. Peirce's contention that the systematicity of nature is a regulative matter of scientific attitude rather than a constitutive matter of scientific fact. Charles Sanders Peirce, *Collected Papers*, Vol. 7 (Cambridge, Mass: Harvard University Press, 1958), sec. 7.134.

as temperature and magnetic forces, then one must design a more complex data-gathering apparatus to take readings over this enlarged range of physical parameters. Or again, in a curve-fitting situation, compare the thesis that the appropriate function is linear with the thesis that it is linear up to a point and sinusoidally wavelike thereafter. Writing a set of instructions for checking whether empirically determined point coordinates fit the specified function is clearly a vastly less complex – and so more economical – process in the linear case. The comparatively simpler is simply that which is easier to work with, which overall is the more economical to operate when it comes to application and interaction. Simplicity on such a perspective is a concept of the practical order, pivoting simply on being more economical to use – that is, less demanding of resources.

Throughout, the key principle is that of economy of means for the realization of given cognitive ends, and the ruling injunction is that of cognitive economy – of getting the most effective answer we can with the least effect of complication. Complexities cannot be ruled out, but they must always pay their way in terms of increased systemic adequacy! And so economy and its other system-definitive congeners – simplicity, uniformity, and the rest – are the natural guidelines. To be sure, whether the direction in which they point us is actually correct is something that remains to be seen. But they clearly afford the most natural and promising starting point. The simplest feasible resolution of our problems is patently that which must be allowed to prevail, at any rate pro tem, until such time as its untenability becomes manifest and complications force themselves upon us. Where a simple solution will accommodate the data at hand, there is no good reason for turning elsewhere. It is a fundamental principle of rational procedure, operative just as much in the cognitive domain as anywhere else, that from among various alternatives that are anything like equally well qualified in other regards, we should adopt the one that is the simplest, the most economical in whatever modes of simplicity and economy are relevant.

Galileo wrote: "When therefore I observe a stone initially at rest falling from a considerable height and gradually acquiring new increases of speed, why should I not believe that such increments come about in the simplest, the most plausible way?"[2] Why not indeed?

---

[2] Galileo Galilei, *Dialogues Concerning Two New Sciences*, trans. H. Crew and A. de Salve (Evanston: University of Illinois Press, 1914), p, 154.

Subsequent findings may, of course, render this simplest position untenable. But this recognition only reinforces the stance that simplicity is not an inevitable hallmark of truth (*simplex sigillum veri*), but merely a methodological tool of inquiry – a guidepost of procedure. When something simple accomplishes the cognitive tasks in hand as well as some more complex alternative, it is foolish to adopt the latter. After all, we need not presuppose that the world somehow is systematic (simple, uniform, and the like) to validate our penchant for the systematicity of our cognitive commitments.

It could, of course, be objected that if presumption is indeed a matter of rational economy of process, then this is going to be something variable through the contrast between (say) economy of time in contrast to economy of effort – with the result that simplicity-presumption can be enormously variable. But this does not mean that it founders as a whole, but only that it cannot be used in those cases when a viable mode of simplicity determination cannot be identified. Presumption is no more a ubiquitous matter of one-resource-soils-it-all than is anything else.

It warrants stress that our striving for cognitive systematicity in its various forms persists even in the face of complex phenomena: the commitment to simplicity in our account of the world remains a methodological desideratum regardless of how complex or untidy the world may turn out to be. We favor uniformity, analogy, simplicity, and the like because this lightens the burden of cognitive effort. When other things are anything like equal, simpler theories are bound to be economically more advantageous. We avoid needless complications whenever possible, because this is the course of an economy of effort. And just herein lies the justification of induction. For by its very nature induction affords us the most cost-effective – the economically optimal – means for accomplishing an essential cognitive task. With cognitive as with physical tools, complexities, disuniformities, abnormalities, and so on are complications that exact a price, departures from the easiest resolution that must be motivated by some appropriate benefit, some situational pressure. Accordingly, it is clear that from this perspective too the rationale of the principles of presumption that characterize our praxis in context of inquiry is a fundamentally economic one.

The informative benefits of knowledge relate to the intrinsic value of having and using information. Besides these costs and benefits of

Positives	Negatives
Comprehensiveness (informativeness)	Narrowness (uninformativeness)
Completeness	Incompleteness
Probability	Improbability
Generality	Particularity
Coherence (fit, inner consistency)	Incoherence (dissonance)
Simplicity	Complexity
Uniformity	Disuniformity
Connectedness	Disjointedness
Elegance	Cumbersomeness
Robustness	Fragility

DISPLAY 9.2. Structural advantages and disadvantages of information

knowledge, there are also certain structural costs and benefits implicit in information-economic features of the body of (purported) knowledge itself, in contrast to the informative services that it provides us. These structural values of information embrace factors like generality, comprehensiveness, completeness, uniformity, simplicity, coherence, and elegance – or on the negative side, fragmentedness, limitedness, incompleteness, disuniformity (eccentricity), complexity, and dissonance. Benefits here relate to the intrinsic economy or elegance, and costs to the intrinsic complexity and cumbersomeness of the information at issue (Display 9.2).

The penchant for inductive systematicity reflected in the structural dimension of information is simply a matter of striving for economy in the conduct of inquiry. We need answers to our questions about the world and the process of getting there is governed by an analogue of Occam's razor – a principle of parsimony to the effect that needless complexity is to be avoided. Given that the inductive method, viewed in its practical and methodological aspect, aims at the most efficient and effective means of question resolution, it is only natural that our inductive precepts should direct us toward the most systematic, and thereby economical, device that can actually do the job at hand. Our systematizing procedures pivot on this injunction always to adopt the most economical (simple, general, straightforward, etc.) solution that meets the demands of the situation. The root principle of inductive systematization is the axiom of cognitive economy: *complicationes non multiplicandae sunt praeter necessitatem*. The other-things-equal preferability of simpler solutions over more complex ones in scientific matters is thus obvious enough: they are less cumbersome to store, easier to take hold of, and less difficult to work with. The presumptions at work here are, as usual, undergirded by a rationale of economy – of utility and convenience.

From this perspective, then, simplicity-preference emerges as an instrument for the simplification of labor, a matter of the intellectual economy of cognitive procedure. Why use a more complex solution when a simple one will do as well? Why depart from uniformity? Why use a new, different solution when an existing one will serve? The good workman selects his tools with a view to (1) their versatility (power, efficacy, adaptability, and the like), and (2) their convenience (ease of use), and other similar factors of functional adequacy to the task in hand.[3] Simplicity preference, accordingly, emerges as a means of implementing the precepts of economy of operation in the intellectual sphere. Its initial advantages are not substantive/ontological but methodological/pragmatic in orientation. The crucial fact is that simplicity preference is a cognitive policy recommended by considerations of cost effectiveness; in the setting of the cognitive purposes at issue, it affords a maximally advantageous inquiry mechanism.

3. Trans-Scientific Presumption

When we turn from science to philosophy we also encounter a manifold of rules of presumption. For with any question in this domain, there is a logical sequence of metaquestions that one can ask about it:

1. Is it *semantically meaningful*: are its terms of reference cogently defined and its concepts intelligible? If so, then –
2. Is it *substantively meaningful*: are the supposed facts on which it is predicated actually true? It so, then –

---

[3] To be sure, these two factors can come into conflict, in which case one must balance things out to see where the weightier considerations lie.

3. Is it *in principle resolvable*: does it fail to be an insolubilium which, on grounds of general principle, does not admit an appropriate answer, so that, at least in theory, it admits of a resolution? If so, then –

4. Is it *tractable*: are we able to secure the information needed to resolve it *in practice*?

In sum, any philosophical question that we can hope to answer faces the series of hurdles indicated by the four conditions at issue. The question will be in trouble in one way or another if it fails at any one of these hurdles. And it is just here that presumptions once more come upon the scene.

To be sure, various schools of philosophy – anti-philosophy – have arisen over the years which hold that the questions of some domain (metaphysics is usually taken as the prime venue) are systematically inappropriate. We thus obtain four positions

- *Radical Skepticism*: The traditionally contemplated questions of the domain are *semantically meaningless*.
- *Moderate Skepticism*: The traditionally contemplated questions of the domain are *substantively meaningless*.
- *Agnosticism*: The traditionally contemplated questions of the domain are *in principle irresolvable*.
- *Scientism*: The traditionally contemplated questions of the domain do not admit of resolutions by the only effective means at our disposal, namely, scientific inquiry.

Against this negativistic background it is clear that a serious commitment to philosophy as a venture in rational cognition is predicated on a fundamental *Presumption of Feasibility* in relation to those four questions – to presuming that the questions of the field are tractable and thereby meaningful and in principle resolvable. In this way, not just the substance of any particular philosophical teaching but the very process of philosophizing is itself predicated on a fundamental enabling presumption. Admittedly, this presumption, like any other, is in principle defeasible. But like any other, it stands firmly in place until actually defeated. Here too the Peircean maxim obtains: One should never bar the path in inquiry.

4. Presumption and the Judgment of Elites

To see the processes and principles of presumption at work within the domain of evaluative judgment it is useful to consider our actual practice with respect to elites.

Elites arise whenever there is a group within whose membership there is some feature of more or less. They consist of those group members who exhibit this feature to a greater extent than most. To symbolize this we shall designate by $< F, G>$ the elite constituted by the subgroup of those G members who exhibit the feature F to a greater than ordinary extent.

However, the special focus on the present discussion will be upon *reflexive* groups – those among whose membership certain intra-group relations obtain, so that some of them can stand in relation R to others. With such a group there will (or can) be

1. The active elite $<R^{\rightarrow}, G>$ consisting of those G-members that R a more than ordinarily larger number of others.
2. The passive elite $<R^{\leftarrow}, G>$ consisting of those G-members that are Rd by a more than ordinarily larger number of others.

With reflexive groups there will accordingly be second-order elites – for example, the people most trusted (or resented) among those who are themselves most trusted (or resented). This second-order elite may be designated by $<R^{\leftarrow}, <R^{\leftarrow}, G\gg$.

Let the reflexive group G consist of $A, B, C,$ plus a couple of others (say D, E). We can now contemplate a relation tabulation to indicate who Rs whom as per

	A	B	C	$[D, E]$
A			√	
B			√	
C	√	√		
$[DE]$				

Thus A Rs C alone, as does B, while C Rs both A and B. Such a tabulation can obviously also be viewed inversely to identify items that are Rd by A or B or C and so on. (We suppose too that there are a couple of further items beyond ABC, but that the tabular entries are always blank there.) Then with the particular relation R at issue with this tabulation the $<R^{\leftarrow}, G>$ elite will consist of C alone because it is the only item Rd by more than an ordinarily larger number of members of G. But what about the second-order elite $<R^{\leftarrow}, <R^{\leftarrow}, GG\gg$? Are there any items that are Rd by a more than ordinary number of $<R^{\leftarrow}, G>= \{C\}$ members? Well yes, there are two of them, namely, A and B.

Various instructive lessons follow. In particular, second-order elites are thus something decidedly different from ordinary elites. Specifically,

1. $<R^{\leftarrow}, <R^{\leftarrow}, GG\gg$ need *not* be a subset of $<R^{\leftarrow}, G>$.
2. $<R^{\leftarrow}, <R^{\leftarrow}, GG\gg$ need *not* be smaller than $<R^{\leftarrow}, G>$.

Again, consider the R-relation given by

	A	B	C	D	E
A			√	√	
B			√	√	
C	√	√			
D	√	√			
E	√	√			

Here we have the elite $<R^{\leftarrow}, G>= \{A, B\}$ seeing that C, D, E all R both A and B. On the other hand $<R^{\leftarrow}, <R^{\leftarrow}, GG\gg =<R, \{A, B\} >= \{D, E\}$ which shares no member with $<R^{\leftarrow}, G>= \{A, B\}$. All in all, then, second-order elites are something quite different from ordinary first-order elites.

POSITIVE
- admired (people)
- cited (articles)
- discussed (themes or topics)
- trusted (people)
- useful (processes)

NEGATIVE
- despised (people)

NEUTRAL
- allocated to others (pieces of metal)

DISPLAY 9.3. Some evaluative elite-establishing features

Within reflexive groups, elites will be either positive or negative depending on the positivity or negativity of the defining relationship at issue. Some examples are given in Display 9.3. As this indicates, what is at issue with second-order elites comes to the set of those who are the most Rd by those who themselves are the most Rd. Following are some examples of evaluative second-order elites:

- The papers most referenced by the papers that are themselves the most referenced
- The people most respected by the people who are themselves the most respected
- The people most discussed by people who are themselves the most discussed
- The people deemed experts (i.e., as being among the most knowledgeable) by people deemed experts
- The people paid the most by the people who are themselves paid the most
- The processes most used within the processes that are themselves the most used
- The film reviewers most highly rated by the most highly rated film reviewers

Most of the above exemplify *positive* second-order elites with the qualifying criterion for the generative base as something that is to be assessed positively. There are also, however, negative reflexive elites – for example, the persons most despised by the persons who are themselves the most despised. Further examples of negative generative bases are the most hated, feared, distrusted, and envied.

The cardinal thesis of the present deliberation is the contention that *normativity comes into operation with positive second-order elites*. We thus arrive at the following thesis:

(*T*) With positive elites factuality can engender normativity in that being Rd to a greater extent than the ordinary seems to establish being; *justifiably Rd*.

With evaluatively positive elites the move to second-order elites is valuation justifying that the valuation at issue is now not just claimed but is such that its ascription comes to be validated.

Thus,

- among people, those esteemed by the most esteemed are indeed esteemable.
- among articles, those cited by the most cited are important (citation-worthy).
- those people deemed expert by those deemed expert deserve to be seen as experts.

Accordingly, the thesis at issue claims that the status being conceded is deserved, that those so classified are *rightly* so classified. What is at issue is a Principle of Elite Authentication to the effect that the correlative endorsements of evaluatively positive elites can be considered appropriate.

To reemphasize: normativity here supervenes on factuality. So in this perspective thesis *T* thus has the striking feature of effecting a transit

- from subjectivity to objectivity
- from factuality to normativity

But how can this be? What is the justificatory rationale of this boundary-crossing thesis *T*?

What is it that entitles those more than ordinarily admired (respected, praised) by those who themselves are admired to a more than ordinary extent to be seen as admirable, respect-deserving, praise-worthy, and so on? Seemingly this is not a merely empirical report on how things go in the world. Nor is such a linkage between perception and value a conceptual one (as J. S. Mill problematically envisioned between being desired and desirability). Something rather different is going on.

What is operative here is to all appearances a generally accepted working hypothesis – a *standing presumption* projected against a variety of supportive experience and grounded in a pivotal need to effect evaluations in matters of the sort at issue. For the reality of it is that the sort of support afforded by thesis *T* is the best sort of support that we will be able to get. In the final analysis it is a matter of practicalistic faute de mieux: the reality is that our best available pathway to people's *being* qualified in judgmental matters proceeds through a consensuality in *being regarded* as such. What better evidence could we ask for in practice in establishing someone's credentials as a bona fide expert than being so acknowledged to a more than ordinary extent by those themselves so regarded to a more than ordinary extent? But of course what is at issue here is not an established fact but a plausible presumption. And so in matters of this sort we once again see at work the now familiar principle that presumption tracks the needs of praxis.

There are various particular and more narrowly focused contexts in which more specific sorts of presumptions play a significant role. And the following chapters will examine some rather striking instances of this phenomenon.

10

Specificity Prioritization and the Primacy of the Particular

1. Specificity Prioritization

The story is told that Herbert Spencer said of Thomas Buckle (or was it the other way round? – as it could just as well have been) that his idea of a tragedy was a beautiful theory destroyed by a recalcitrant fact. A fundamental epistemic principle is at issue here, namely, that when the limited particularity of fact and the broad generality of theory come into conflict in the case of otherwise plausible propositions, then it is the former that will prevail. Facts, as the proverb has it, are stubborn things: in case of a clash, facts must prevail over theories, observations over speculations, concrete instances over abstract generalities, limited laws over broader theories. With factual issues specificity predominates generality when other things are anything like equal. And so a far-reaching Principle of Specificity Precedence comes into view with respect to rational inquiry.

The workings of such a Principle of Specificity Precedence can be illustrated from many different points of view. The practice of monitoring hypothetical theorizing by means of experimentation is characteristic of the scientific process, and the Principle of Specificity Precedence is fundamental here. Throughout, whenever speculation clashes with the phenomena, a conjectured hypotheses with the data at our disposal, or a theory with observation then it is generally – and almost automatically – the former that is made to give way.

Presumption, that is to say, stands on the side of specificity throughout the realm of factual inquiry.

This circumstance obtains not only in clashes between observation with theory but also in clashes between a lower level (less general or abstract) theory with one that is of a higher (more general and abstract) level. Here too the comparatively specific rival will prevail in situations of conflict. And the general principle prevails with the historical sciences every bit as much as from the sciences of nature. A single piece of new textual evidence or a single item of new archeological discovery can suffice to undo a conflicting theory. A penchant for specificity preference is very much in operation.

Philosophy affords yet another illustration of specificity preference. The work of Thomas Reid (1710–96) and the philosophers of the Scottish school he typifies illustrates this in an especially vivid way. These thinkers reasoned as follows: suppose that a conflict arises between some speculative fact of philosophical theorizing and certain more particular, down-to-earth bits of everyday common sense. Then it of course will and must be those philosophical contentions that must give way.

In just this spirit, Reid insisted that common sense must hold priority over the more speculative teaching of philosophy. Maintaining that most philosophers themselves have some sense of this he observes wryly that "it is pleasant to observe the fruitless pains which Bishop Berkeley took to show that his system . . . did not contradict the sentiment of the vulgar, but only those of the philosophers."[1] Reid firmly held that any clash between philosophy and common sense must be resolved in the latter's favor. Should such a clash occur,

the philosopher himself must yield . . . [because] such [commonsense] principles are older, and of more authority, than philosophy; she rests upon them as her basis, not they upon her. If she could overturn them she would become buried in their ruins, but all the engines of philosophical subtlety are too weak for this purpose.[2]

In any conflict between philosophy and everyday commonsense beliefs it is the latter that must prevail. The down-to-earth lessons of ordinary

---

[1] *Essays on the Intellectual Powers of Man* (Edinburgh: John Bell, 1785), Vol. VI, iv, p. 570.

[2] *An Inquiry into the Human Mind* (1764), Vol. I, v (ed. William Hamilton, p. 102b; ed. Edward Brooks, p. 21).

experience must always prevail over any conflicting speculations of philosophical theorizing. On this point the Scottish commonsensists were emphatic: when conflicts arise, commonplace experience trumps philosophical speculation. And in fact most metaphilosophical accounts of philosophizing agree with this specificity-favoring point of view.

Yet another illustration of specificity preference comes (perhaps surprisingly) from pure mathematics. In deliberating about the relationship between mathematics proper and metamathematical theorizing about mathematical issues, the great German mathematician David Hilbert (1862–1943) also argued for specificity preference. If any conflict should arise between substantive mathematical findings and large-scale metamathematical theory, so he maintained, then it is automatically the latter that must yield by way of abandonment or modification. Here too we are to favor concrete specificity over abstract generality: seeing that, across a wide range of mathematics, abstract metamathematical theories are comparatively more risky. Accordingly, consider what Arthur Fine calls "Hilbert's Maxim," namely the thesis that

metatheoretic arguments [about a theory] must satisfy more stringent requirements [of acceptability] than those placed on the arguments used by the theory in question.[3]

And so the mathematical realm can afford yet another illustration of specificity preference. It appears that throughout our inquiry into the reality of things the pursuit of knowledge prioritizes specificity. Presumption, that is to say, stands on the side of comparative specificity and definiteness.

2. The Rationale of Specificity Prioritization

Is there a cogent rationale for this? Are there sound reasons of general principle why specificity should be advantaged?

---

[3] See Arthur Fine, "The Natural Ontological Attitude," in Jarret Leplin (ed.), *Scientific Realism* (Berkeley and Los Angeles: University of California Press, 1984), pp. 83–107 (see esp. p. 85). The maxim was articulated in line with David Hilbert's endeavor to demonstrate the consistency of set theory on a more concrete non-set-theoretical basis.

An affirmative answer is clearly in order here. The reasoning at issue runs somewhat as follows. Consider a conflict case of the sort that now concerns us. Here, in the presence of various other uncontested "innocent bystanders" (x), we are forced to a choice between a generality (g) and a specificity (s) because an inferential situation of the following generic structure obtains:

$$(g \& x) \to \sim s \text{ or equivalently } (s \& x) \to \sim g$$

It is thus clear that with the unproblematic context x fixed in place, either s or g must be sacrificed. But since g, being general, encompasses a whole variety of other special cases – some of which might well also go wrong – we have, in effect, a forced choice occasioned by a clash between a composition complex and a competition of very limited scope. And since the extensiveness of the former affords a greater scope for error, the latter is bound to be the safer bet. As a rule, generalities are probatively more vulnerable than specificities. When other things are anything like equal, it is clearly easier for error to gain entry into a larger than into a smaller manifold of claims.

In cases of conflict or contradiction in our information, the cognitive dissonance that needs to be removed is to be resolved in favor of the more particularly concrete, definite party to the conflict. The more general, the more cases are included, and so the more open to error: generality is a source of vulnerability, and when clashes arise, particularity enjoys priority. We have to presume that specifics are in a better probative position than generalities because they are by nature easier to evidentiate, seeing that generalities encompass a multitude of specifics. Contrariwise, seemingly established generalities are easier to disestablish than specifics because a single counterinstance among many possibilities will disestablish a generality, whereas it takes something definite to disestablish a particularity. And perhaps another reason it is easier to make a generality yield to a specificity is that damage control is easier with generalities, where matters can often be put to rights by minor readjustments and tinkerings, while with specifications there is less room for maneuver. But this of course is simply yet another aspect of the rational economy of procedure that is determinative for presumption.

Accordingly, it transpires that ordinarily and in "normal" circumstances, specificities are on safer ground and thereby enjoy probative precedence in situations of discord and inconsistency. When information is being distilled into coherent knowledge, we presume the correctness of the more specific so that specificity prioritization is the rule.

To be sure, it must be acknowledged that specificity preference is not a matter of a propositional truth-claim but a procedural principle of presumption. What is at issue is not a factual generalization to the effect that specificities inevitably prevail over generalities, but a precept of epistemic practice on the order of "Believe the testimony of your own eyes" or "Accept the claim for which the available evidence is stronger." It is a matter of the procedural principle. And of course one can possibly go wrong here: it is not true that what your eyes tell is always so or that the truth always lies on the side of the stronger evidential case in hand. All that we have – and all that is at issue – is that such methodological processes of rational procedure afford a process that will generally lead us aright. Though not infallible, they are good guides to practice in affording us general adequacy rather than failproof correctness. And the justification at issue is thus one of functional efficacy – of serving the purposes of the practice at issue effectively. Here, as elsewhere, presumption is less a matter of demonstrating a universal truth than of validating a procedural practice on the basis of its general effectiveness.

3. A Curious Inversion: The Case of Counterfactuals

In factual matters – for example, "inductive" reasoning in science – we prioritize specific facts over generalities in cases of a forced choice. It is, however, necessary to come to terms with the striking circumstance that there is an important family of cases where the more usual presumption of specificity prioritization is in fact inverted and in the reverse process a generality prioritization obtains. This occurs when we are dealing not with matters of fact, but with fact-contradicting assumptions and hypotheses.[4] For here exactly the reverse policy is in

---

[4] On counterfactual conditionals and their problems, see N. Rescher, *Hypothetical Reasoning* (Amsterdam: North Holland, 1964) and *Imagining Irreality* (Chicago:

order and a Principle of Generality Preference obtains that privileges laws over particular descriptive facts.[5] In these matters theory and practice alike conspire to indicate that considerations of nomic uniformity are paramount and that lawfulness, commonality, normality, and their congeners are in the driver's seat.[6] It is the pivotal role of systemic fundamentality in counterfactual reasoning that marks this as a matter less of abstract rationality and logic than of common sense.

By way of illustration, contrast the following counterfactuals:

If he had thrown the switch, the light would have gone on (because that's how the system is designed to work).

If he had thrown the switch, nothing would have happened (because the connection is broken).

Open Court, 2000). See also David Lewis, *Counterfactuals* (Oxford: Blackwell, 1973); Ernest Sosa (ed.), *Causation and Conditionals* (London: Oxford University Press, 1975); Anthony Appiah, *Assertion and Conditionals* (Cambridge: Cambridge University Press, 1985); Frank Jackson (ed.), *Conditionals* (Oxford: Clarendon Press, 1991).

[5] This principle was initially articulated in Rescher, "Belief-Contravening Suppositions," *Philosophical Review*, Vol. 20 (1961), pp. 176–95, and further expounded in his *Hypothetical Reasoning* (Amsterdam: North Holland, 1964) and *Imagining Irreality* (Chicago: Open Court, 2000). For empirical substitution of the theory see the next footnote.

[6] Not only does this have the backing of a sound rationale of theoretical analysis, but a whole host of empirical studies coalesce to indicate that people in fact think in this way. See R. Revlis, S. G. Lipkin, and J. R. Hayes, "The Importance of Universal Quantifiers in a Hypothetical Reasoning Task," *Journal of Verbal Learning and Verbal Behavior*, 10 (1971): 86–91; R. Revlis, and J. R. Hayes, "The Primacy of Generalities in Hypothetical Reasoning," *Cognitive Psychology*, 3 (1972): 268–90; H. H. Kelley, and J. Michaela, "Attribution Theory and Research," *Annual Review of Psychology*, 31 (1980): 457–501; Daniel Kahneman and A. Tversky, "The Simulation Heuristic," in Kahneman, P. Slovic, and A. Tversky (eds.) *Judgment under Uncertainty* (Cambridge: Cambridge University Press, 1982), pp. 201–8; J. T. Johnson, "The Knowledge of What Might Have Been: Affective and Attributional Consequences of Near Outcomes," *Personality and Social Psychology Bulletin*, 12 (1986): 51–62; Daniel Kahneman and D. T. Miller, "Norm Theory: Comparing Reality to Its Alternatives," *Psychological Review*, 93 (1986): 136–53; Neal J. Roese, and James M. Olsen, "Self-esteem and Counterfactual Thinking," *Journal of Personality and Social Psychology*, 65 (1993): 199–206; Igor, Gavanski and G. L. Wells, "Counterfactual Processing of Normal and Exceptional Events," *Journal of Experimental Social Psychology*, 25 (1989): 314–25; and D. T., Miller, W. Turnbull, and C. McFarland, "Counterfactual Thinking and Social Perception: Thinking about What Might Have Been," in M. P. Zanna (ed.), *Advances in Experimental Social Psychology*, Vol. 23 (Orlando, Fla. Academic Press, 1990), pp. 305–31, as well as the many relevant studies cited by these authors.

Of course if we *know* the connection is broken, the second counterfactual wins out. But absent such knowledge, the first prevails. And for good reason. For the issue is one of normalcy versus malfunction.

Beliefs:

1. He did not throw the switch.
2. The light did not go on.
3. Whenever the switch is thrown, the light goes on.

Assumption:

Not-(1): He threw the switch.

To resolve consistency in the face of the assumption, either (2) or (3) must be jettisoned. And in prioritizing the lawful (3) over the merely factual (2), we had best maintain the lawfully general, "normal" order of things.

By way of further illustration, consider the counterfactual question:

If this rubber band were made of copper, what then?

It is clear that this question arises in an epistemic context where the following beliefs are salient:

Beliefs:

1. This band is made of rubber.
2. This band is not made of copper.
3. This band does not conduct electricity.
4. Things made of rubber do not conduct electricity.
5. Things made of copper do conduct electricity.

Let it be that we are now instructed to accept the hypothesis:

Not-(2): This band is made of copper.

Then the following two propositional sets are the hypothesis-compatible maximal consistent subsets of our specified belief-set:

$\{(3), (4)\}$ corresponding to the acceptance/rejection
         alternative (3), (4)/(1), (2), (5)

$\{(4), (5)\}$ corresponding to the acceptance/rejection
         alternative (4), (5)/(1), (2), (3)

The first alternative corresponds to the counterfactual

> If this band were made of copper, then copper would not conduct electricity [since this band does not conduct electricity].

And the second alternative corresponds to the counterfactual

> If this band were made of copper, then it would conduct electricity [since copper conducts electricity].

In effect we are driven to a choice between (3) and (5), that is, between a particular feature of this band and a general fact about copper things. However, its greater generality qualifies (5) as being systemically more informative, and its prioritization is therefore appropriate. Accordingly, we will retain (4) and (5) along with not-(2), and therefore accept that second counterfactual as appropriate. And this exemplifies a general situation of generality preference in matters of counterfactual reasoning.

And so, as this example illustrates, *in deliberating with respect to fact-contradicting assumptions, generality precedence comes into play.* We arrive at a larger lesson. In determining which beliefs should give way in the face of counterfactual assumptions we do and should let informativeness be our guide, so that authentic generality is now in the driver's seat.[7] Rational procedure in speculative contexts becomes a matter of keeping our systemic grip on the manifold of relevant information as best we can.

4. Natural versus Unnatural Counterfactuals

Again, consider the question "What if Booth had not murdered Lincoln?" And let us suppose that the salient beliefs here stand as follows:

1. Lincoln was murdered in April 1865.
2. Murder is deliberate killing so if Lincoln was murdered, it was by someone deliberately trying to kill him.
3. Booth murdered Lincoln.
4. Only Booth was deliberately trying to kill Lincoln in April 1865.

---

7 In this context, it is, however, important that the generalization at issue be seen as somehow lawful and as not a merely fortuitous and accidental aggregation of special cases, so that the factor of generality is present in name only.

Observe that (1), (2), and (4) entail (3). Now suppose not-(3). To achieve consistency we must now abandon one of the trio: (1), (2), (4). Here (2) is a definitional truth. And (4) is a general fact, while (1) is but a matter of specific fact. The rule of precedence for matters of generality/informativeness marks (1) as the weakest link and we arrive at this:

> If Booth had not murdered Lincoln, Lincoln would not have been murdered in April 1865.

In a similar vein, we have the problem of explaining how the subjunctively articulated counterfactual

> If Oswald had not shot Kennedy, then nobody would have.

seems perfectly acceptable, while the corresponding indicative conditional

> If Oswald did not shoot Kennedy, then no one did.

seems deeply problematic.[8] And within the presently contemplated frame of reference the answer is straightforward. The background of accepted belief here is as follows:

1. Kennedy was shot.
2. Oswald shot Kennedy.
3. Oswald acted alone: No one apart from Oswald was trying to shoot Kennedy.

Now suppose that (2) is replaced by its negation not-(2), that is, that Oswald had not shot Kennedy. For the sake of consistency we are then required to abandon either (1) or (3). And the informativeness-geared policy of presumption via generality precedence in matters of mere hypothesis now rules in favor of retaining (3), thus dropping (1) and arriving at the former of that pair of conditionals. The alternative but inappropriate step of dismissing (1), would, by contrast, issue in that second, decidedly implausible counterfactual.

To be sure, this conditional could in theory be recast in a more complex form that would rescue it as it were:

---

[8] This issue is addressed in E. W. Adams, "Subjective and Indicative Conditionals," *Foundations of Language*, 6 (1970): 39–94.

If Oswald did not shoot Kennedy, then no one did; so since Kennedy was shot, Oswald did it.

In this revised version the conditional in effect constitutes a *reductio ad absurdum* of the idea that Oswald did not shoot Kennedy. But it is now clear that these conditionals address very different questions, namely the (1)-rejecting

What if Oswald had not shot Kennedy?

and the (1)-retaining

Who shot Kennedy?

respectively. With conditionals as with factual statements, the question being addressed becomes a pivotal consideration.

The distinction between "natural" and "unnatural" counterfactuals is, of course, crucial in the present context. To illustrate this, let us suppose that we know that all the coins in the till are made of copper. Then we can say without hesitation:

If the coin I have in mind is in the till, then it is made of copper.

But we certainly cannot say counterfactually

If the coin I have in mind were in the till, then it would be made of copper.

After all, I could perfectly well have a certain silver coin in mind, which would certainly not change its composition by being placed in the till.

But just how is the difference between the two cases to be explained? Let $C = \{c_1, c_2, \ldots, c_n\}$ be the set of coins in the till, where by hypothesis all of these c_i are made of copper. And now consider the assumption:

Let x be one of the c_i (that is, let it be some otherwise unspecified one of those coins presently in the till).

Clearly this assumption, together with our given "All of the c_i are made of copper," will entail "x is made of copper" so that first conditional is validated.

But in the second case we merely have the assumption

Let x be a coin in the till (through not necessarily one of those presently there).

Now, of course, this hypotheses joined to "All of the coins presently in the till are made of copper," will obviously not yield that conclusion. Accordingly, the second counterfactual is in trouble, since the information available to serve as its enthymematic basis is insufficient to validate the requisite deduction. The two conditionals are different because they involve different assumptions of differing epistemic status, a difference subtly marked by use of the indicative in the first case and the subjunctive in the second. For in the former we are dealing merely with *de facto* arrangements, while in the latter case with a lawful generalization. And so generality prioritization speaks for the latter alternative. Lawfulness makes all the difference here, for generality precedence is now in play.

To be sure, in the case of a counterfactual supposition that is itself particular we may have to make a generalization give way to it. This arises standardly in the case of thought experiments contemplating outcomes that may defeat generalizations. Thus consider the following counterfactual relating to testing the generalization (g) that heavy objects (like rocks) fall to earth when released:

If this heavy rock had not fallen to earth when it was released at altitude yesterday, then generalization g would be false.

Here we have the following beliefs to the facts of the situation:

1. That heavy rock was released at altitude yesterday.
2. That rock then fell to earth.
3. Heavy objects (like rocks) fall to earth when released at altitude (= generalization g).

When now instructed to assume not-(2), the resulting inconsistency forces a choice between abandoning the specific (1) and the general (3). With automatic generality precedence one would be constrained to retain (3) and jettison (1). But that of course is not how things work in such a thought experiment. For now the particular thesis at issue, namely (1), is here immunized against rejection by the fact of its constituting part of the very hypothesis at issue.

5. The Key Lesson

What is thus crucial with counterfactuals is how certain principles of precedence and priority function to guide the determination of right-of-way for restoring consistency in cases of conflict. For we proceed here on the basis of this rule:

In counterfactual reasoning, the right-of-way priority among the issue-salient beliefs is determined in terms of their generality of import by way of informativeness in the systemic context at hand.

In counterfactual contexts, generalities accordingly take precedence over specificities. Once we enter the realm of fact-contravening hypotheses, those general theses and themes that we subordinate to specifics in factual matters now become our life preservers. We cling to them for dear life, and do all that is necessary to keep them in place. "Salvage as much information about the actual condition of things as you possibly can" is now our watchword. Accordingly, specifics and particularities will here yield way to generalizations and abstractions.

The situation can be summarized in the unifying slogan that in hypothetical situations the standard modus operandi of presumption prioritizes beliefs on the basis of *systematicity preference*. But this matter of right of way is now determined with reference to informativeness within the wider context of our knowledge. When we play fast and loose with the world's facts we need the security of keeping its fundamentals in place. Once we enter the realm of fact-contravening hypotheses and suppositions, then those general truths and theories become more passable. And so now, specifics and particularities yield way to generalizations and abstractions.

On this basis, it is standard policy that *in counterfactual contexts, propositions viewed as comparatively more informative in the systemic context at hand will take priority over those that are less so.* While revisions by way of curtailment and abandonment in our family of relevant belief are unavoidable and inevitable in the face of belief-countervailing hypotheses, we want to give up as little as possible. And here the ruling principle is, "Break the chain of inconsistency at its weakest link in point of systemic informativeness." And this in turn provides for generality preference. For in determining which beliefs are to give way in the face of counterfactual assumptions we do and should let informativeness be our guide. Keeping our systemic grip on the manifold of relevant information is the crux, and speaks clearly for generality-precedence here.

6. Conclusion

The lesson of these deliberations is clear. When a clash among seemingly acceptable propositions occurs in *factual* contexts, the relevant modes of plausibility and presumption lead us to adopt the stance of specificity-preference. But in *counterfactual* contexts where the economics of information conservation is paramount, our deliberations are subject to generality preference at issue with systemic cogency. In matters of conflict within the factual domain, presumption lies on the side of specificity, while in the speculatively counterfactual domain it favors lawful generality. In the larger scheme of things, two diametrically opposed principles – specificity prioritization and generality prioritization – are in operation in our overall deliberations. But they obtain in very different sectors of the cognitive terrain – namely, factual inquiry and counterfactual speculation. And in both cases alike, it is the purposive nature of the enterprise that determines the appropriateness of the correlative prioritization principle.

The crux of the matter is that here once again the purposive manifold of the particular area of deliberation at issue constitutes the decisive factor. With factual inquiry we aim at the security of our cognitive commitments and accordingly opt for the greater evidential security of specificity as the more reliable guide. By contrast, with counterfactual reasonings we look for the results of disbelieved hypotheses and will advantage generalities because we strive to retain the maximum of information that survives the turmoil produced in our cognitive commitments through the impact of discordant assumptions. And so, here, as elsewhere, it is the difference in the aims and purposes characteristic of the enterprise at hand that accounts for the difference in the procedural process that is appropriate.

Throughout all settings in which presumption plays a role – inquiry, communication, and social interaction preeminently included – the same fundamental factor is at work: *rational economy*. Presumption, as we have seen, is always something of a leap in the dark. It involves a risk that we are prepared to run for the promise of goal attainment.

But in the calculation of cost and benefit characteristic of all, rational praxis is once again critical here. The principles of presumption are part and parcel of rational economy – of the effect to principle the realization of objectives in the manner which, on balance, affords the most cost-effective prospects in relation to the enterprise at hand.

11

Dismissing Extremely Remote Possibilities

1. Introduction

Theorists of knowledge have long recognized and emphasized that there are significant differences between theoretical and practical reason, between problem solving in purely theoretical matters (where nothing is at stake save the possibility of mistaken beliefs), and in practical matters (where actual harm of some sort might be incurred). There is, perhaps, no more striking illustration of this situation than the little heeded issue of the treatment of very remote possibilities – those whose probability is *extremely* small. Here the question before us is this: in regard to matters of practice, should a diminutive probability (one of an effectively infinitesimal magnitude ϵ) be seen as being indistinguishable from zero and treated as having no magnitude at all? In deploying probabilities in expected-value comparisons that serve as guides for decision making, could and should we adopt the equation: $\epsilon = 0$?[1] Are we to dismiss those minute probabilities and presume them to be zero? Sometimes the answer is a decided affirmative. And this chapter accordingly addresses one very special case of presumption that answers in relation to our planning for the future, namely, the dismissal of diminutively far-fetched possibilities from our reckoning.

---

[1] Some of the issues of this chapter were also discussed in Rescher, *Risk* (Lanham, Md.: University Press of America, 1983); see especially pp. 35–40. I am grateful to Ben Eggleston for constructive comments.

2. Effectively Zero Probabilities

Probability and cognitive presumption are closely interconnected. The step from probability to presumption is mediated by the consideration that when answers are needed the probability of the available alternatives can help to provide guidance. And the step from presumption to probability is mediated by the consideration that if we deemed a certain answer impracticable, we would not presume it.

A probability has to be a quantity between zero and one. Now numbers between zero and one can get to be very small indeed: As N gets bigger, $1/N$ will grow very, very small. What, then, is one to do about those extremely small probabilities in the rational management of risks?[2]

On this issue there is something of a professional disagreement between probabilists working on theory-oriented issues in mathematics or natural science and decision theorists who work on practical issues relating to human affairs. The former take the line that small numbers are small numbers and must be taken into account as such – that is, as the small quantities they actually are. The latter tend to take the view that small probabilities represent an extremely remote prospect and can be written off. (*De minimis non curat lex*, as the old legal precept has it: in human affairs there is no need to bother with trifles.) When something is about as probable as that a thousand fair dice when tossed a thousand times will all come up sixes, then, so it is held, we can pretty well forget about it as worthy of concern. As a matter of practical policy we operate with probabilities on the principle that for suitably small $\in$, when $x < \in$, then $x = 0$. We take the line that in our human dealings in real-life situations a sufficiently remote possibility can – for all sensible purposes – be presumed to be of probability zero.

Accordingly, such remote possibilities can simply be dismissed, and the outcomes with which they are associated can accordingly be set

---

[2] Recent probability theorists concerned with inductive issues have dealt with infinitesimal probabilities almost exclusively in the context of the probability of scientific generalizations and laws. (See Richard C. Jeffrey, *The Logic of Decision*, 2nd ed. (Chicago & London: University of Chicago Press, 1983), pp. 190–95; and John Earman, *Bayes or Bust* (Cambridge, Mass.: MIT Press, 1992) pp. 86–95). This issue of the epistemic acceptability of propositions is of course something rather different from that of the action-guiding concerns of decision theory.

aside. And in "the real world" people do in fact seem to be prepared to treat certain probabilities as effectively zero, taking certain sufficiently improbable eventualities as no longer representing *real* possibilities.[3] Here an extremely improbable event is seen as something we can simply write off as being "outside the range of appropriate concern," something we can dismiss for "all practical purposes." As one writer on insurance puts it:

People . . . refuse to worry about losses whose probability is below some threshold. Probabilities below the threshold are treated as though they were zero.[4]

No doubt, remote-possibility events having such a minute possibility *can* happen in some sense of the term, but this "can" functions somewhat figuratively, it is no longer seen as something that presents a realistic prospect.

In epistemic contexts, as David Lewis has pointed out, the assignment of probability zero or one indicates "absolute certainty [that] is tantamount to a firm resolution never to change your mind, no matter what."[5] However, in the practicalistic use of decision theory in contexts of choosing courses of action, setting a probability at zero means no more than ruling out the corresponding possibility provisionally, pro tem, as an object of appropriate concern in the situation at hand. Thus in practical contexts, such a treatment of the probabilities at issue is essentially a matter of fiat – of deciding that as a matter of policy a certain level of sufficiently low probability can be taken as a cut-off point below which we are no longer dealing with "*real* possibilities" and with "*genuine* risks." The significance of such a probability-annihilating presumption is something rather different in these two contexts of deliberation: what is *absolute* certainty in the one is no more than *practical* certainty in the other.

---

3 In theory this idea of a threshold of effective zerohood can lead to anomalies when the whole spectrum of possibility is covered by a mass of such improbable eventuations. The so-called Lottery Paradox is an example. See Henry E. Kyburg, Jr., *Probability and the Logic of Rational Belief* (Middletown, Conn.: Wesleyan University Press, 1961.) But this theoretical worry is rendered harmless by the fact that most real-life situations do not take this problematic form. (Compare also Sect. 4 later in the chapter.)

4 Paul Slovic et al., "Preference for Insuring against Probable Small Losses: Insurance Implications," *Journal of Risk and Insurance*, 44 (1977): 237–258 (see p. 254).

5 David Lewis, "Causal Decision Theory," *Australasian Journal of Philosophy*, 59 (1981): 14.

For, of course, this recourse to effective zerohood does not represent a strictly objective, factual circumstance. (After all, $\epsilon = 0$ is a literal falsehood.) It reflects a matter of choice or decision, namely, the *practical* step of treating certain theoretically extant possibilities as unreal – as not worth bothering about, as being literally *negligible* and meriting being set at zero. It is not that those minimalities do not exist, but that we need not trouble ourselves about them because of the improbability of matters going wrong. We can, in brief, dismiss them from the range of practical concern. After all, we are operating with issues in the practical rather than theoretical domain.

It thus needs to be emphasized that $\epsilon = 0$ is not being adopted as a factual contention and thereby as involving us in a useful error (*felix culpa*) of some sort. It is not a matter of a convenient, albeit erroneous claim, but of a *practical policy* procedure. The situation is akin to that of presumptions like "In the absence of specific counterindications, accept what people say as true." Taken as a thesis of fact (with that ACCEPT AS deleted) the claim is false. But it can, nevertheless, prove to be useful and productive as a practical policy.

3. How Small Is Small Enough?

Of course, the question remains: How small is small enough for being "effectively zero"? With what value of ϵ does the presumption that $\epsilon = 0$ begin to take hold: just exactly where does the threshold of effective zerohood lie?

This is clearly not something that can be resolved in a once-and-for-all manner. It will presumably vary from case to case as, for example, with the magnitude of the stake at issue. For it seems plausible to allow the threshold of effective zerohood to reflect the magnitude of the threat at issue, taking lower values as the magnitude of the stake at issue increases. Thus the empirical conditions seem to indicate that in deliberating about risks to human life, for example, there is some tendency to take as a baseline a person's chance of death by natural disasters (or "acts of God"), roughly $1/1,000,000$ per annum in the United States. This would be seen as something akin to the "noise level" of a physical system, and fatality probabilities significantly smaller than this would thus be seen as negligible. Such an approach seems to underlie the Food and Drug Administration's proposed, rather more conservative standard of "1 in 1 million over a lifetime."[6] People's stance in the face of the probability that when embarking on a commercial airplane trip they will end up as an aviation fatality (which stood at roughly one in 300 million in the United States prior to 9/11/01) also illustrates this perspective. (In such matters, most people neither worry nor will they insure unless "the company pays.")

However, one important point must be noted in this connection. The probability values that we treat as effectively zero must be values of which, in themselves, we are very sure indeed. But real-life probability values are seldom all that precise. And so in general there will be considerable difficulty in sustaining the judgment that a certain probability indeed is effectively zero. A striking instance is afforded by the Atomic Energy Commission-sponsored "Rasmussen report" of the 1970s (named after Norman C. Rasmussen, the study director) on the accident risks of nuclear power plants:

From the viewpoint of a person living in the general vicinity of a reactor, the likelihood of being killed in any one year in a reactor accident is one chance in 300,000,000 and the likelihood of being injured in any one year in a reactor accident is one chance in 150,000,000.[7]

The theoretical calculations that sustain such a finding invoke so many assumptions regarding facts, circumstances, and operating principles that such probability estimates are extremely shaky. Outside the domain of purely theoretical science we are too readily plunged below the threshold of experimental error and will thus confront great difficulties in supporting minute probability distinctions in the sphere of technological and social applications. Statistical probabilities can be very problematic in this regard, in particular since statistical data are often deficient or unavailable in the case of very rare events. Personal

---

[6] U.S. Food and Drug Administration, "Chemical Compounds in Food-processing Animals. Criteria and Procedures for Evaluating Assays of Carcinogenic Residues" (Washington, D.C.: U. S. Government Printing Offices March 20, 1979; 44 *Federal Register*, 17070–114.)

[7] U.S. Atomic Energy Commission [U.S. Nuclear Regulatory Commission], *An Assessment of Accident Risks in U.S. Commercial Nuclear Power Plants* (Washington, D.C.: U. S. Government Printing Offices 1974); summary volume AEC Publication WASH-1400 (Aug., 1974). Quoted in William W. Lowrance, *Of Acceptable Risk* (Los Altos: Kaufmann, 1976), p. 73.

probabilities – mere guesses, that is to say – are also very vulnerable in this context of assessing very low probabilities. (For example, the flood victims interviewed by the geographer R. W. Kates flatly denied that a flood could ever recur in their area, erroneously attributing previous floods to freak combinations or circumstances that were extremely unlikely to recur.)[8] One writer has maintained that in safety engineering contexts it simply is not possible to construct sufficiently convincing arguments to support very small probabilities (below 10^5).[9] Moreover, it is sometimes tempting to exaggerate the extent to which a distinct possibility is remote. And indeed a diversified literature has been devoted to describing the ways in which the estimation of very low probabilities can go astray.[10] So there is ample room for due caution in this regard.[11]

4. Why Accept a Threshold of "Effective Zerohood"?

The idea of treating very small probabilities as effectively zero goes back a long way – to Buffon in the eighteenth century and Cournot in

---

[8] R. W. Kates, "Hazard and Choice Perception in Flood Plain Management," Research Paper No. 78, Department of Geography, University of Chicago, 1962.

[9] J. P. Holdren, "The Nuclear Controversy and the Limitations of Decision Making by Experts," *Bulletin of the Atomic Scientists*, 32 (1976): 20–22.

[10] G. W. Fairley, "Criteria for Evaluating the 'Small' Probability of a Catastrophic Accident from the Marine Transportation of Liquefied Natural Gas," in D. Okrent (ed.), *Risk-benefit Methodology and Application: Some Papers Presented at the Engineering Foundation Workshop, Asilomar* (Los Angeles: University of California, Department of Energy and Kinetics, UCLA-ENG 7598; 1975); Baruch Fischoff, "Cost-benefit Analysis and the Art of Motorcycle Maintenance," *Policy Sciences*, 8 (1977): 177–202; A. E. Green and A. J. Bourne, *Reliability Technology* (New York: Wiley-Interscience, 1972); Paul Slovic, "Behavioral Decision Theory," *Annual Review of Psychology*, 28 (1977): 1–39; A. Tversky and D. Kahneman, "Judgment under Uncertainty: Heuristics and Biases," *Science*, 185 (1974): 1124–1131.

[11] This ambivalent situation was noted already by Jean Le Rond d'Alembert (1717–83). On the one hand he endorsed the principle that a diminutive mathematical probability should be seen as effectively zero: "quand la probabilité d'un événement est fort petite, elle doit être regardée et traité comme nulle" (*Reflexions sur le calcul des probabilités*, art 10 [*Opuscules mathématiques*], Vol. 2 10ème Mémoire (Paris: David, 1761). On the other hand, securely fixing the potentiality of an identifiable event at so small a magnitude is effectively impossible, so that "d'assigner la loi de cette [miniscule] diminution, c'est ce que ni moi, ni personne, je crois, ne peut pas faire" (*Doutes et questions sur le calcul des probabilités* [1767], Oeuvres (Paris: Belin, 1812;), Vol 7, pp. 451–62).

the nineteenth.[12] This stratagem treats certain eventuations as *moral impossibilities* and their nonrealization as *moral* certainties (in the traditional terminology, for which one might substitute the designation of *practical*). The original motivation for adopting a threshold of effective zerohood arose out of Daniel Bernoulli's "St. Petersburg paradox" set by the following imaginary game:[13]

A fair coin is to be tossed until a head appears. If it does so on the nth toss, the gambler is then to be paid 2^n ducats. How much should the gambler be prepared to pay to enter the game?

It is easy to see that the mathematical expectation of this gamble is

$$\sum_{n=1}^{\infty} (2^n) \times (1/2)^n$$

which is clearly infinite. So by the usual standards the gambler should be willing to pay any finite stake, however large. This is clearly counterintuitive. And so Buffon proposed to resolve this problem by emphasizing that the probability $(1/2)^n$ soon becomes very small indeed for increasing n. Once the stage is reached where these small-probability eventuations are seen as "effectively impossible," the mathematical expectation of return becomes finite, and the paradox is resolved.

There are, to be sure, other and perhaps better ways of overcoming this particular obstacle.[14] But there are also other pressing reasons

---

[12] See Theirry Martin, *Probabilités et critique philosophique selon Cournot* (Paris: Vrin, 1990), who discusses under the title of "Cournat's principle" the idea that events of small potentiality are rare – and the smaller, the rarer. Martin vigorously opposes Cournot's idea that a minute probability – however small – can ever be set at zero or indicate a "physical compossibility." (See Martin, *Probabilités*, Chap. 5, pp. 171–237.) At best and at most we can, at our own risk, *decide* to *treat* small-potentiality events as being impossible but this is now a *psychological* (or "moral") rather than a *physical* (or "ontological") impossibility. See also Kenneth J. Arrow, "Alternative Approaches to the Theory of Choice in Risk-Taking Situations," *Econometrica*, 19 (1951): 404–37 (see p. 414).

[13] Bernoulli's original 1738 essay "Specimen theoriae novae de mensura sortis" has been translated into English in *Ecomometrica*, 22 (1954): 23–36, into German by A. Pringsheim as *Versuch einer neuen Theorie von Glücksfällen* (Leipzig: Duncker und Humblot, 1896), and also into various other languages.

[14] See Richard Jeffrey, *The Logic of Decision*, 2nd ed. (Chicago and London: University of Chicago Press, 1983), pp. 151–55. The classical approach of Bernoulli himself was to conduct the evaluative process in terms of utility rather than money, envisioning the utility of money to decline exponentially with amount. Another approach is to deploy Herbert Simon's conception of satisficing with its view that "enough is enough." See

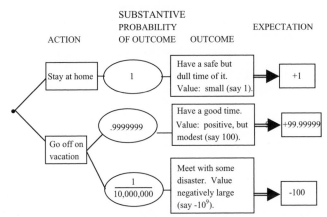

DISPLAY 11.1. *The Vacationer's Dilemma. Note:* The expectation here is the product of the probability of the outcome times its value. Thus for the bottom line we have $10^{-7} \times 10^9 = -100$.

for dismissing sufficiently improbable possibilities. One of them lies in our need and desire to avoid stultifying action. It is simply "human nature" to dismiss sufficiently remote eventualities in one's personal calculations. After all, there are just too many of them to cope with in practical terms. To be asked to reckon with such remote possibilities is to baffle our thought by sending it on a chase after endless alternatives.

Then too, heeding remote possibilities is an invitation to stultifying inaction. The "Vacationer's Dilemma" of Display 11.1 illustrates this phenomenon. Dismissing sufficiently remote catastrophic misfortunes as lying outside the range of *real* possibilities – by treating them as negligible – is clearly one effective means for averting the stultification of inaction when proceeding on the standard decision-making approach represented by expected-value calculations. The vacationer takes the plausible line of viewing the chance of disaster as effectively zero, thereby blocking that unacceptable possible outcome from intimidation. People generally (and justifiably) proceed on the assumption that

Michael A. Slote, *Beyond Optimizing* (Cambridge, Mass.: Harvard University Press, 1989). Mathematical aspects of the problem are addressed in Emile Borel, *Valeur pratique et philosophie des probabilités* (Paris: Gauthier-Vellers, 1939).

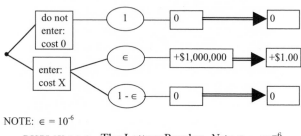

NOTE: $\in = 10^{-6}$

DISPLAY 11.2. The Lottery Perplex. *Note:* $\in = 10^{-6}$

the probability of sufficiently unlikely disasters can be set at zero; that in certain common-life contexts unpleasant eventuations of extreme improbability can be dismissed as lying outside the realm of "*real*" or "*genuine*" possibilities. Fretting about extremely remote possibilities – even of quite substantial disasters – simply makes life too difficult.[15] So here fitness considerations seem to favor the dismissal of extremely remote possibilities, seeing that this enables us to keep our practice within the framework of expectation-based decision theory without having to take anomalous and counterintuitive results in stride. For a reliance on the standard mechanisms of decision theory will in some circumstances no longer be sensible unless we are prepared to dismiss extremely small probabilities as zero.[16] Without some such practical policy, mathematical expectation is no longer a safe and sensible guide to rational decision in such extreme situations.

To be sure, there are also situations in which we incur a disadvantage when we set $\in = 0$. Thus consider the situation of Display 11.2, which pictures the situation of a person confronted with the choice of paying $\$X$ to enter a lottery with a one-in-a-million chance of winning a prize of a million dollars or abstaining from this gamble. Since the expected value of entering is $\$1.00$, the subject would, on classical principles, be

[15] It is also possible to entertain the idea of utter catastrophes conceived of as "unacceptable" possibilities that one would not be prepared to risk under any circumstances – no matter how small the possibility of their realization. But this poses different issues and leads into other directions than those presently in view.

[16] On the opposite side of the coin lies the distinction between mere disasters and outright catastrophes – the latter being eventuations so horrendous that we would in no circumstances accept any course of action that involves a probability of realization greater than genuine zero. On this issue see Rescher, *Risk* (Lanham, Md.: University Press of America, 1983), pp. 75–76.

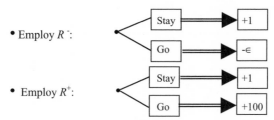

DISPLAY 11.3. The Vacationer's Dilemma at the methodological level

enjoined to enter the lottery if the cost of doing so were 99¢ (or less). On the other hand, if we adopted the idea of setting $\in\, = 0$ then the expected value comparison will balance out at 0, so that on classical decision principles our agent would be entirely indifferent between the alternatives.

On expected value principles, in the Vacationer's Dilemma the subject would seemingly forgo a highly probable benefit in the face of risks of infinitesimally improbable disaster. But in the Lottery Perplex our subject is led by this policy to the prospect of paying a sure (albeit modest) price for the sake of an opportunity for a substantial albeit most improbable gain. The idea of setting $\in\, = 0$ does not look all that attractive from this latter standpoint. So here too we have a matter of choice.

5. The Question of Validation

The very issue before us can itself be viewed in a decision-theoretic perspective. In addressing such decision problems we implicitly also confront a second-order decision problem, namely that of deciding whether to employ the policy R^+ of setting $\in\, = 0$ or to employ the policy R^- of not doing so. Proceeding at this point in the orthodox way we make the expected-value calculation in both ways and then compare. Thus consider the situation of the Vacationer's Dilemma in the methodological perspective of Display 11.3. Viewed on this basis the second alternative clearly looks better than the first on grounds of dominance, so that R^+ is in order.

But by contrast consider the structure of the Lottery Perplex as per Display 11.4. Here the first alternative looks to be more attractive than the second, seeing that enter or not, we fare comparatively better by

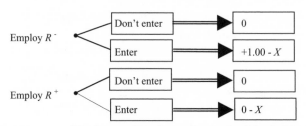

<small>DISPLAY 11.4. The Lottery Perplex at the methodological level</small>

following its counsel. And so R^- obtains the advantage and is in order in this case.

The point is that the issue of setting $\in\, = 0$ can itself be regarded as a (second order) decision problem posing an issue of procedural choice in certain situations, and this decision problem can, as such, be translated by the standard decision-theoretic means.

6. Overcoming a Problem

To be sure, a further worry looms on the horizon. For the fact of it is that a substantial accumulation of minute chances can become significant.[17] Thus if we systematically and routinely take the step of setting $\in\, = 0$ for diminutive $\in$, then consider a vast roulette wheel with a zillion compartments, so that the probability that the outcome will lie in any given compartment is less than some diminutive $\in$. But now consider the probability that the outcome will be in one or another of these compartments. Since that roulette ball will have to wind up somewhere, this quantity is clearly 1. But on the other hand the probability of any particular compartment is some $\in$ which is set at zero and $0 \times$ (anything) $= 0$. So on this basis the above-mentioned probability is 0. Our policy of setting diminutive probabilities to zero has plunged us into a contradiction.[18] The point is that large intervals can be traversed by the repetition of small steps and that if one sets minute

---

[17] The German proverb has it that "Kleinvieh macht auch Mist." More seriously, a wide spectrum of trivially small risks can become collectively nontrivial, which is why people go to Lloyds for insurance.

[18] This situation mirrors that of the so-called Lottery Paradox, which was originally formulated in H. E. Kyburg, Jr., *Probability in the Logic of Rational Belief* (Middleton, Conn.: Wesleyan University Press, 1961).

distances to zero, then their repetition – no matter how many – will still be zero on the standard arithmetical principle that 0 x n = 0. How is one to come to terms with this inconsistency?

The solution lies in taking the bull by the horns in stipulating that the step of equating ∈ with 0 is permissible *only once* within the overall context of any particular decision problem.[19] For to do this repeatedly would be a matter of having too much of a good thing. Here as elsewhere overindulgence can prove the road to disaster. For a proposition claiming an outcome whose probability becomes 1 when we set ∈ = 0 will be said to be *virtually certain.* And as the Lottery Paradox shows, a conjunction of such propositions may *or may not* itself turn out to be virtually certain.

Accordingly, we can now lay claim to the following principle of practical deliberation:

In a course of practical reasoning – but here only – it is acceptable to include among the premises one – but only one! – proposition that is no more than virtually *certain.*

Sometimes, to be sure, a number of cases can be folded into one. But not always and everywhere – and specifically not in such damaging cases as those that engender problems of the sort at issue in the Lottery Paradox.

It may seem odd to contemplate a rule of procedure that can be used only a limited number of times. But an analogy may help to make this situation more plausible. Consider the rule of practice at issue in the abbreviative convention: in writing omit every fourth letter (counting a space as a letter). Let us apply this rule to the sentence at the beginning of this section.

IT∗<u>MAY</u>∗<u>SEEM</u>∗<u>ODD</u>∗TO∗<u>C</u>ONT<u>E</u>MPL<u>A</u>TE ∗ <u>A</u> ∗ RU<u>L</u>E OF∗
PRO<u>C</u>EDU<u>RE</u>

In implementing that suppression rule one arrives at

IT ∗ AY ∗ EEMODDTO ∗ ONTEMPLTE ∗ ∗RUEOPROEDUE

Here it is (perhaps just) possible for a reasonably clever person to figure out what is being said. But it can be left as an exercise for the

---

[19] This proviso will require setting the boundaries for what is to be a single decision context. But this issue, while not without its difficulties, involves ultimately manageable complexities that lead beyond the limits of the present deliberations.

reader to verify that matters are reduced to a hopeless condition when the rule is applied twice over in dealing with the same text. In just this way, the policy of setting $\epsilon = 0$ is something that must be employed not only with caution and discretion but with rarity. And the reason for that once-only qualification is substantially the same in both cases, namely, that the compromise of information involved in repeated use of the rule is too large. Each repeated use further muddies the informative waters so that repetition becomes inappropriate. In both cases alike we have an instance of an otherwise viable practice that can be stretched too far – a practical resource whose *repeated* use may, rather than being helpful, work to defeat the purpose at hand.

7. Conclusion

The lesson of these deliberations is that the status of the thesis $\epsilon = 0$ is not that of an established truth but rather that of a presumption. But this presumption of effective zerohood must – like many another – be made with caution. As usual with presumptions it is defeasible: clearly we cannot always and everywhere proceed on the basis that $\epsilon = 0$. We can proceed on its basis for "as long as we can get away with it." But when it leads us into difficulties we are revealed as fair-weather friends, and abandon it without scruple. Yet this does not mean that we should not expect to get away with it on many occasions. And just here lies the crux of the matter: the resort to effective zerohood inherent in the equation $\epsilon = 0$ in these decision-theoretic matters is not a conjectured fact but a defeasible presumption whose basis – like that of all presumptions – lies in its systemic utility in the wider setting of our practical concerns.

After all, in life we have to take risks. And a ruling maxim of sensible procedure here is inherent in the following practical policy:

If proceeding *X*-wise is advantageous or convenient and only very rarely leads to error or difficulty, then it is sensible and appropriate to proceed in this way.

As is the case with other presumptions, setting $\epsilon = 0$ follows under exactly this practical policy – indeed is something of a quintessential instance of its operation.

In the final analysis, then, three sorts of decision situations need to be distinguished:

- *Unproblematic situations* where the standard process of expected value comparison can be applied in the usual way.
- *Totally catastrophic situations* where there are risks we would not want to run no matter how small the probability invoked.
- *Extremely remote probability situations* of the "ordinary" sort in which we would choose to apply the dismissive ($\epsilon = 0$) tactic as contemplated here.

The really vexing problem is that of deciding how to proceed in situations that fall into both of the last two categories where two conflicting principles are at work: to dismiss extremely remote possibilities and never to accept the risk of catastrophe. For the dilemma here is that there is unfortunately no way to achieve an easy resolution on principles of abstract reason alone. We pays our money and takes our choice – and then have no alternative but to live with the consequences. In guiding our decisions, effective zerohood is no more than a defeasible presumption. Given the realities regarding our choices in the management of practical affairs, this is the best that we can possibly do, so that here, as elsewhere, it makes no sense to ask for more. In the end, practical reason has no rational alternative but to proceed with the limits that theoretical reason imposes. And because presumption is always to some extent a leap in the dark, one must acknowledge that in such matters calculation must always leave some room for common sense. And in the end, resolution that is needed here has to be made on the basis of what is no more (but also no less) than a judgment call.

Of course, things may, very possibly, go wrong in such matters. But only rarely. "And surely" – so we would reflect "not in the particular case presently at hand." And the validation of such ϵ-probability dismissal makes perfect sense by its own lights. It is, in fact, a self-justifying policy. Nor is this regrettable. After all, any really fundamental epistemic process must prove to be self-supportive in the final analysis. And here, in the present instance, self-support is not defect but rather a virtue.

Conclusion

Most philosophical theorists of knowledge – the classical rationalists (like Descartes and Spinoza) and empiricists (like Hume) as well as various later thinkers from Brentano to our contemporaries – have been concerned primarily with knowledge in the sense of *what we know for certain.* In consequence it has transpired that – apart from forays by mathematically oriented theorists such as F. P. Ramsey, J. M. Keynes, and R. Carnap into the domain of probability – contemporary epistemology has almost wholly neglected the range of conceptions in the region of uncertainty, the gray area of concepts that, like presumption and plausibility, have an indecisively tentative impetus toward truth.

The quest for certainty has continued to exercise a virtually hypnotic fascination on contemporary theorists of knowledge, who have, accordingly, tended to neglect cognitive claims that stop short of pretentions to definitive finality. But by rights epistemology should surely be seen as having a far broader range, concerned not just with knowledge as such but with a great variety of cognitive matters such as belief, conjecture, supposition, and much else. And it is just here – in the theory of cognition at large – that the concept of presumption comes into its own and provides a healthy antidote to the fundamentalist epistemologies whose inadequacy to provide an adequate theoretical basis for rational inquiry has become increasingly evident in recent years. The topic is accordingly a timely one because there is nowadays increasing interest among philosophers and cognitive theorist in such issues as vagueness and conjecture that manifest the workings of rational communication and inquiry under the sub-ideal conditions of imperfect information.

Since there is always a reason why behind a reason why, the process of rational inflection never achieves categorical closure. And it is precisely because of this that presumption is particularly important, seeing that it alone among rational processes enables us to resolve issues whose evidentiation has not as yet reached the end of an ultimately incompletable journey.

The situation was not always as it has become. In classical antiquity the idea of presumption played a large part in the theory of knowledge, although the terminology was different. The concept of *prolepsis* (generally translated "preconception," but effectively tantamount to a "natural presumption") was introduced by Epicurus and played a prominent part in the epistemological controversies between the Epicurean and Stoic schools.[1] And in fact those ancient ideas still continue to have considerable promise for dealing with a great variety of issues bearing on the nature and validation of knowledge. After all, even if we focus our interest upon knowledge alone we must recognize that knowledge does not come *ex nihilo* but emerges from a background of supposition, presumption, conjecture, assumption, and so on, and that the nature of knowledge cannot be properly apprehended without coming to terms with these as well.

The tendency of philosophers to neglect the role of rationally warranted presumptions can be illustrated by reference to K. R. Popper's interesting discussion of the uniformity-of-nature principle. He wrote:

When Kant said that our intellect imposes its laws upon nature, he was right – except that he did not notice how often our intellect fails in the attempt: the regularities we try to impose are *psychologically* a priori, but there is not the slightest reason to assume that they are [*probatively*] a priori valid, as Kant thought. The need to try to impose such regularities upon our environment is, clearly, inborn, and based on drives or instincts. There is the general need for a world that conforms to our expectations.[2]

---

[1] One informative recent discussion is F. H. Sandbach, "Ennoia and Prolepsis in the Stoic Theory of Knowledge," in A. A. Long (ed.), *Problems in Stoicism* (London: Athlone Press, 1971), pp. 22–37.

[2] K. R. Popper, *Objective Knowledge* (Oxford: Clarendon Press, 1972), pp. 23–4.

One rather striking aspect of this passage is its emphatic disjunctiveness: the principle of regularity-subsumption is *either* a factual thesis (in which case it lacks adequately supportive warrant) or else merely a psychologically grounded stipulation (in which case it is probatively irrelevant). But from our present standpoint, this dichotomy is gravely deficient. For distinct and apart from the factual claim and the psychological tendency there also stands the epistemic policy of rational presumption.

While presumption has always played an important role in legal reasoning and in the theory of disputation, it has been unduly neglected in cognitive theory and in philosophical epistemology. And this is unfortunate because the concept affords an instrument whose considerable power and utility comes to the fore in various sectors of the cognitive domain.

For the concept of a rationally warranted presumption provides a resource that opens up new and fertile epistemic vistas. After all, epistemology has to be seen as more inclusive and ample than the theory of *knowledge* because its overall range encompasses also such issues as probability and plausibility, where our claims to truth are not categorical but hedged. And presumption in particular is a salient resource of cognition quite different alike from factual knowledge and psychological penchant.

The fact of it is that we can and do operate effectively with presumptions in many areas of rational endeavor, not only in law and in everyday life (as is familiar and well known) but also in science and in philosophy. Presumption is a versatile cognitive instrumentality that serves us well in a broad spectrum of epistemic applications. And as the present deliberations have shown, this approach has deep roots in a theoretical rationale that underpins the processes of rational inquiry and communication.

One of the principal services afforded us by a recourse to presumptions lies in its affording the basis for a dynamic theory of knowledge – one that does not simply begin with putative truths obtained *ex nihilo*, but rather sees the knowledge acquisition as a process of moving from tentative presumption to ultimate acceptance. The concepts of plausibility and presumption provide the means for a characteristically variant, nonfoundationalist approach to probative reasoning that sees knowledge development as a continuous upgrading of fallible materials rather than as a two-phase process of extracting inferential knowledge from immediate and supposedly self-evident knowledge of some sort.

Overall, then, presumption serves an important and eminently useful resource for cognition. And it does so both because its deliverances play a crucial role in informational gap filling and because they provide the materials needed to get the cognitive project off to a start in the first place. Without the resources of presumption the project of rational inquiry and communication would not just be substantially impoverished but would be virtually hamstrung.

Bibliography

Adams, E. W. "Subjective and Indicative Conditionals." *Foundations of Language*, 6 (1970): 39–94.

d'Alembert, Jean Le Rond. *Reflexions sur le calcul des probabilités*, art 10 [*Opuscules mathématiques*], Vol. 2 10ème Mémoire. Paris: David, 1761.

Almeder, Robert. "Fallibilism and the Ultimate Irreversible Opinion." In *Essays in the Theory of Knowledge*, edited by N. Rescher, pp. 33–54. Oxford: Basil Blackwell, 1975; *American Philosophical Quarterly* Monograph, no. 9.

Appiah, Anthony. *Assertion and Conditionals*. Cambridge: Cambridge University Press, 1985.

Aristotle. *Topics*. Cambridge, Mass.: Harvard University Press, 1939.

Aristotle. *On Sophistical Refutations* (De Sophisticis Elenchis), translated by E. S. Forster. Cambridge, Mass.: Harvard University Press, 1955.

Arrow, Kenneth J. "Alternative Approaches to the Theory of Choice in Risk-Taking Situations." *Econometrica*, 19 (1951): 404–37.

Audi, Robert. *Practical Reasoning*. New York: Routledge, 1989.

Axelrod, Robert. *The Evolution of Cooperation*. New York: Basic Books, 1984.

Bach, Kent. "Default Reasoning." *Pacific Philosophical Quarterly*, 65 (1984): 37–58.

Bacon, Francis. *Novum Organon*.

Bernoulli, Daniel. "Specimen theoriae novae de mensura sortis," translated into German by A. Pringsheim as *Versuch einer neuen Theorie von Glücksfällen*. Leipzig: Duncker & Humblot, 1896.

Berkeley, George. *Essays on the Intellectual Powers of Man*. Edinburgh: John Bell, 1785.

Blanshard, Brand. *The Nature of Thought*. London: Macmillan, 1939.

Borel, Emile. *Valeur pratique et philosophie des probabilités*. Paris: Gauthier-Vellers, 1939.

Braithwaite, R. B. *Scientific Explanation*. Cambridge: Cambridge University Press, 1953.

Brewka, Gerhard. *Nonmonotonic Reasoning: Logical Foundation of Common Sense.* Cambridge: Cambridge University Press, 1991.

Campbell, Richmond and Lanning Sowden (eds.). *Paradoxes of Rationality and Cooperation.* Vancouver: University of British Columbia Press, 1985.

Campbell, S. K. *Flaws and Fallacies in Statistical Thinking.* Englewood Cliffs: Prentice Hall, 1974.

Chisholm, Roderick M. "Law Statements and Counterfactual Inference." *Analysis*, 15 (1955): 97.

Chisholm, Roderick M. *The Problem of the Criterion.* Milwaukee: Marquette University Press, 1973.

Clarke, D. S., Jr. *Practical Inferences.* London: Routledge, 1985.

Clarke, D. S., Jr. *Rational Acceptance and Purpose.* Totowa, N.J.: Rowman and Littlefield, 1989.

David, Morton D. *Game Theory.* New York: Basic Books, 1970.

Davidson, Donald, and Gilbert Harman (eds.), *The Logic of Grammar.* Encino, Calif.: Dickenson, 1975.

Degnan, R. E. "Evidence." *Encyclopedia Britannica*, 15th ed., Vol. 8 (1963), pp. 905–16.

Descartes, René. *Meditations on First Philosophy*, No. 1. Trans. R. M. Eaton.

Earman, John. *Bayes or Bust.* Cambridge, Mass.: MIT Press, 1992.

Eeinemen, F. H. Van. *Fundamentals of Argumentation Theory.* (Mahwah, N.J.: Lawrence Erlbaum, 1996.

Eisler, Rudolf. *Handwörterbuch der Philosophie*, 2nd ed. Berlin: E. S. Mittler & Sohn, 1922.

Epstein, Richard A. "Pleadings and Presumptions." *University of Chicago Law Review*, 40 (1973/4): 556–82.

Ewing, A. C. *Idealism: A Critical Survey.* London: Macmillan, 1934.

Fairley, G. W. "Criteria for Evaluating the 'Small' Probability of a Catastrophic Accident from the Marine Transportation of Liquefied Natural Gas." In *Risk-benefit Methodology and Application: Some Papers Presented at the Engineering Foundation Workshop, Asilomar*, edited by D. Okrent. Los Angeles: University of California, Department of Energy and Kinetics, UCLA-ENG 7598; 1975.

Fine, Arthur. "The Natural Ontological Attitude." In *Scientific Realism*, edited by Jarret Leplin, pp. 83–107. Berkeley and Los Angeles: University of California Press, 1984.

Fischoff, Baruch. "Cost-benefit Analysis and the Art of Motorcycle Maintenance." *Policy Sciences*, 8 (1977): 177–202.

Galilei, Galileo. *Dialogues Concerning Two New Sciences.* Trans. H. Crew and A. de Salve. Evanston: University of Illinois Press, 1914.

Gaskins, Richard H. *Burdens of Proof in Modern Discourse.* New Haven: Yale University Press, 1992.

Garfinkel, Harold. *Studies in Ethnomethodology.* Englewood Cliffs, N.J.: Prentice Hall, 1967.

Gauthier, David. *Morals by Agreement.* Oxford: Oxford University Press, 1986.

Gavanski, Igor, and G. L. Wells. "Counterfactual Processing of Normal and Exceptional Events." *Journal of Experimental Social Psychology*, 25 (1989): 314–25.

Gazdar, G. *Pragmatics, Implications, Presupposition, and Logical Form.* New York: Academic Press, 1979.

Gerhard, C. I. (ed.). *Die philosophischen Schriften von G. W. Leibniz*, Vol. 3. Berlin: Weidmann, 1887.

Golding, Martin. *Legal Reasoning.* New York: Knopf, 1984.

Gonseth, Ferdinand. "La Notion du normal." *Dialectica* 3 (1947): 243–52.

Goodman, N. *Fact; Fiction and Forecast.* Cambridge, Mass.: Harvard University Press, 1955.

Green, A. E. and A. J. Bourne. *Reliability Technology.* New York: Wiley-Interscience, 1972.

Grice, H. P. "Logic and Conversation." In *The Logic of Grammar*, edited by D. Davison and G. Harman, pp. 64–75. Encino, Calif.: Dickenson, 1975.

Grice, H. P. *Studies in the Ways of Words.* Cambridge, Mass.: Harvard University Press, 1989.

Hall, Roland. "Presuming." *Philosophical Quarterly*, 11 (1961): 10–22.

Hanson, Norwood R. *Patterns of Discovery.* Cambridge: Cambridge University Press, 1958.

Hanson, Norwood R. "Is There a Logic of Discovery?" In *Current Issues in the Philosophy of Science*, Vol. I, edited by H. Feigl and G. Maxwell. (New York: Free Press, 1961).

Hardwig, John. "The Role of Trust in Knowledge." *Journal of Philosophy*, 88 (1991): 693–708.

Harper, William L. "A Sketch of Some Recent Developments in the Theory of Conditionals." In *IFS: Conditionals, Belief, Decision, Chance and Time*, edited by W. L. Harper, L. G. Pearson, and R. Stalnaker. Dordrecht: D. Reidel, 1981.

Hilpinen, R. *Rules of Acceptances and Inductive Logic.* (Amsterdam: North-Holland Publishing, 1968; *Acta Philosophica Fennica*, fasc. 22).

Holdren, J. P. "The Nuclear Controversy and the Limitations of Decision Making by Experts." *Bulletin of the Atomic Scientists*, 32 (1976): 20–22.

Ilbert, Sir Courtenay. "Evidence." *Encyclopedia Britannica*, 11th ed., Vol. 10, pp. 11–21. Cambridge, 1910.

Jackson, Frank (ed.). *Conditionals.* Oxford: Clarendon Press, 1991.

James, William. "The Sentiment of Rationality." In *The Will to Believe and Other Essays in Popular Philosophy.* New York: Longmans Green, 1897.

Jeffrey, Richard C. *The Logic of Decision*, 2nd ed. Chicago & London: University of Chicago Press, 1983.

Joachim, H. H. *The Nature of Truth.* Oxford: Clarendon Press, 1906.

Jones, Burr W. *The Law of Evidence.* San Francisco: Bancroft-Whitney, 1896; 5th ed., 1958).

Kahneman, Daniel, and D. T. Miller. "Norm Theory: Comparing Reality to Its Alternatives." *Psychological Review*, 93 (1986): 136–53.

Kahneman, Daniel, and A. Tversky. "The Simulation Heuristic." In *Judgment under Uncertainty*, edited by Daniel Kahneman, P. Slovic, and A. Twersky, pp. 201–8. Cambridge: Cambridge University Press, 1982.

Kates, R. W. "Hazard and Choice Perception in Flood Plain Management." Research Paper No. 78, Department of Geography, University of Chicago, 1962.

Katzner, Louis I. "Presumptions of Reason and Presumptions of Justice." *The Journal of Philosophy*, 70 (1973): 89–100.

Keffer, H. *De Obligationibus: Relevastrontation einer spätmittelalterlichen Disputationstheorie*. Leiden: Brill, 2001.

Kelley, H. H., and J. Michaela. "Attribution Theory and Research." *Annual Review of Psychology*, 31 (1980): 457–501.

Keynes, Maynard. *A Treatise on Probability*. London: Macmillan, 1921.

Kneale, William. *Probability and Induction*. Oxford: Clarendon Press, 1939.

Kyburg, Henry E., Jr. *Probability and the Logic of Rational Belief*. Middletown, Conn.: Wesleyan University Press, 1961.

Kyburg, Henry E., Jr., and Chon Man Teng. *Uncertain Inference*. Cambridge: Cambridge University Press, 2001.

Lalande, André. *Vocabulaire de la philosophie*, 9th ed. Paris: Presses Universitaires de France, 1962.

Lamb, James W. "Knowledge and Justified Presumption." *Journal of Philosophy*, 69 (1972): 123–27.

Levi, I. *Gambling with Truth*. New York: Knopf, 1967.

Levinson, S. *Pragmatics*. Cambridge: Cambridge University Press, 1983.

Levinson, S. *Presumptive Meanings*. Cambridge, Mass.: MIT Press, 2002.

Lewis, C. I. *An Analysis of Knowledge and Valuation* (La Salle, Ill.: Open Court, 1962).

Lewis, David. "Causal Decision Theory." *Australasian Journal of Philosophy*, 59 (1981): 14.

Lewis, David. *Counterfactuals*. Oxford: Blackwell, 1973.

Lewis, David. *Convention: A Philosophical Study*. Cambridge, Mass: Harvard University Press, 1969.

Llendu, J. E. "Presuppositions, Assumptions, and Presumptions." *Theoria*, 28 (1962): 15–72.

Llewelton, J. E. "Presuppositions, Assumptions, and Presumptions." *Theoria*, 28 (1962): 158–72.

Lowrance, William W. *Of Acceptable Risk*. Los Altos: Kaufmann, 1976.

Martin, Theirry. *Probabilités et critique philosophique selon Cournot*. Paris: Vrin, 1990.

McCarthy, John. "Circumscription—a Form of Non-monotonic Reasoning." *Artificial Intelligence*, 13 (1980): 27–30.

McDermott, D., and J. Doyle, "Non-Monotonic Logic." *Artificial Intelligence*, 13 (1980): 41–72.

Mercer, Robert E. *A Default-Logic Approach to Natural Language Presuppositions*. Vancouver: University of British Columbia, 1987.

Morgan, Edmund M. "Some Observations Concerning Presumptions." *Harvard Law Review*, 44 (1930–31): 906–34.

Morgan, Edmund M. "Instructing the Jury upon Presumptions and Burden of Proof." *Harvard Law Review*, 47 (1933–34): 59–83.

Nagel, Ernest. *The Structure of Science*. New York: Harcourt-Brace-World, 1961.

Parsons, Terence. "A Meinongian Analysis of Fictional Objects." *Grazer Philosophische Studien*, 1 (1974): 73–86.

Parsons, Terence. "A Prolegomenon to Meinongian Semantics." *Journal of Philosophy*, 71 (1974): 551–60.

Peirce, C. S. *Collected Papers*, 8 vols. Cambridge: Harvard University Press, 1931–58.

Perelman, Chaim. *Justice, Law and Argument*. Dordrecht: Reidel, 1980.

Perelman, Chaim, and L. Olbrechts-Tyteca. *The New Rhetoric: A Treatise on Argumentation*, 2nd ed., translated. by J. Wilkinson and P. Weaver. Notre Dame: University of Notre Dame Press, 1969.

Phipson, Sidney L. *The Law of Evidence*. London: Stevens and Haynes, 1892; 11th ed., 1970.

Pollock, J. L. "A Theory of Defeasible Reasoning." *International Journal of Intelligent Systems*, 6 (1991): 33–54.

Popper, K. R. *Objective Knowledge*. Oxford: Clarendon Press, 1972.

Polya, Georre. *Introduction and Analogy in Mathematics*. Princeton: Princeton University Press, 1954.

Polya, Georre. *Patterns of Plausible Inference*. Princeton, 1954.

Rappoport, Anatol. "Escape from Paradox." *American Scientist*, 217 (1967): 50–6.

Rapport, A., and A. M. Chammah. *Prisoner's Dilemma: A Study in Conflict and Cooperation*. Ann Arbor: University of Michigan Press, 1965.

Reid, Thomas. *An Inquiry into the Human Mind*. (1764).

Reid, Thomas. *Essays on the Intellectual Powers of Man*. Edinburgh: John Bell, 1785.

Reiter, Raymond. "A Logic for Default Reasoning." *Artificial Intelligence*, 13 (1980): 81–132.

Reiter, Ray. "Nonmonotonic Reasoning." *Annual Review of Computer Sciences*, 2 (1987): 147–86.

Rescher, Nicholas. "The Illegitimacy of Cartesian Doubt." *Review of Metaphysics*, 13 (1959): 226–34. Reprinted with some revisions in *Essays in Philosophical Analysis* (Pittsburgh: University of Pittsburgh Press, 1969).

Rescher, Nicholas. "Belief-Contravening Suppositions." *Philosophical Review*, 70 (1961): 176–96.

Rescher, Nicholas. *Hypothetical Reasoning*. Amsterdam: North Holland, 1964.

Rescher, Nicholas. *The Coherence Theory of Truth*. Oxford: Clarendon Press, 1973.

Rescher, Nicholas. *The Primacy of Practice*. Oxford: Clarendon Press, 1973.

Rescher, Nicholas. *Plausible Reasoning*. Assen-Amsterdam: Van Gorcum, 1976.

Rescher, Nicholas. *Dialectics: A Controversy-Oriented Approach to the Theory of Knowledge*. Albany: SUNY Press, 1977.

Rescher, Nicholas. *Methodological Pragmatism.* Oxford: Blackwell, 1977.

Rescher, Nicholas. *Peirce's Philosophy of Science.* Notre Dame: University of Notre Dame Press, 1978.

Rescher, Nicholas. *Induction.* Oxford: Basil Blackwell, 1980.

Rescher, Nicholas. *Empirical Inquiry.* Totowa, N.J.: Rowman and Littlefield, 1982.

Rescher, Nicholas. *Risk.* Lanham, Md.: University Press of America, 1983.

Rescher, Nicholas. *Scepticism.* Oxford: Blackwell, 1980.

Rescher, Nicholas. *Cognitive Economy.* Pittsburgh: University of Pittsburgh Press, 1989.

Rescher, Nicholas. *Human Knowledge in Idealistic Perspective.* Princeton: Princeton University Press, 1991.

Rescher, Nicholas. *A Useful Inheritance.* Pittsburgh: University of Pittsburgh Press, 1994.

Rescher, Nicholas. *Imagining Irreality.* Chicago: Open Court, 2000.

Rescher, Nicholas. *Fairness.* New Brunswick, N.J.: Transaction Press, 2001.

Revlis, R., and J. R. Hayes. "The Primacy of Generalities in Hypothetical Reasoning." *Cognitive Psychology,* 3 (1972): 268–90.

Revlis, R., S. G. Lipkin, and J. R. Hayes. "The Importance of Universal Quantifiers in a Hypothetical Reasoning Task." *Journal of Verbal Learning and Verbal Behavior,* 10 (1971): 86–91.

Robinson, R. "Arguing from Ignorance." *Philosophical Quarterly,* 21 (1971): 97–108.

Roese, Neal J., and James M. Olsen, "Self-esteem and Counterfactual Thinking," *Journal of Personality and Social Psychology,* 65 (1993): 199–206.

Ross, Angus. "Why Do We Believe What We are Told?" *Ratio,* 28 (1986): 69–88.

Ross, W. D. *Aristotle's Prime and Posterior Analytics.* Oxford: Clarendon Press, 1949.

Rougier, Louis. *Traité de la connaisance.* Paris: Gauthier-Villars, 1955.

Ruse, Michael. *Taking Darwin Seriously.* Oxford: Blackwell, 1986.

Russell, Bertrand. *The Problems of Philosophy.* New York: Henry Holt, 1912.

Sandbach, F. H. "Ennoia and Prolepsis in the Stoic Theory of Knowledge." In *Problems in Stoicism,* edited by A. A. Long, pp. 22–37. London: Athlone Press, 1971.

Sanders, Gerald H. *Introduction to Contemporary Academic Debate,* 2nd ed. Prospect Heights, Ill.: Waveland Press, 1983.

Scheffler, I. *Science and Subjectivity.* New York. 1967.

Schlick, M. "The Foundation of Knowledge." In *Logical Positivism,* edited by A. J. Ayer, pp. 209–27. Glencoe, Ill., 1959.

Schutz, Alfred. *Der sinnhafte Aufbau der sozialen Welt.* Wien: J. Springer, 1932.

Searle, John. *Speech Acts.* Cambridge: Cambridge University Press, 1969.

Sellars, Wilfred. "Giveness and Explanatory Coherence." *Journal of Philosophy,* 70 (1973).

Sextus Empiricus. *Outlines of Pyrrhonism.*

Simon, Herbert A. "Thinking by Computers" and "Scientific Discovery and the Psychology of Problem Solving." In *Mind and Cosmos,* edited by R. E. Colodny, pp. 115–32. Pittsburgh, 1966.

Slote, Michael, A. *Beyond Optimizing.* Cambridge, Mass.: Harvard University Press, 1989.

Slovic, Paul. "Behavioral Decision Theory." *Annual Review of Psychology,* 28 (1977): 1–39.

Slovic, Paul, et al. "Preference for Insuring against Probable Small Losses: Insurance Implications." *Journal of Risk and Insurance,* 44 (1977): 237–58.

Sosa, Ernest (ed.). *Causation and Conditionals.* London: Oxford University Press, 1975.

Sowell, Thomas. *Knowledge and Decisions.* New York: Basic Books, 1980.

Sperbar, David, and Deirdre Wilson. *Relevance: Communication and Cognition.* Oxford: Basil Blackwell, 1986.

Sproule, J. Michael. "The Psychological Burden of Proof: On the Evolutionary Development of Richard Whately's Theory of Presumption." *Communicative Monographs,* 43 (1976): 115–29.

Stephen, James Fitzjames. *A Digest of the Law of Evidence.* London: Macmillan, 1877.

Stough, Charlotte L. *Greek Skepticism.* Berkeley and Los Angeles: University of California Press, 1969.

Stump, Eleonore, and P. V. Spade. "Obligations." In *The Cambridge History of Later Medieval Philosophy,* edited by Norman Kretzmann, pp. 315–41. Cambridge: Cambridge University Press, 1998.

Thayer, James Bradley. *A Preliminary Treatise on Evidence at Common Law.* Boston: Little, Brown, 1898.

Toulmin, Steven. *The Uses of Argument.* Cambridge: Cambridge University Press, 1958.

Turnbull, W., and C. McFarland, "Counterfactual Thinking and Social Perception: Thinking about What Might Have Been." In *Advances in Experimental Social Psychology,* edited by M. P. Zanna, pp. 305–31. Orlando, Fla.: Academic Press, 1990.

Tuomela, Raimo. *Cooperation.* Dordrecht: Kluwer, 2000.

Tversky, A., and D. Kahneman. "Judgment under Uncertainty: Heuristics and Biases." *Science,* 185 (1974): 1124–131.

Ullmann-Margalit, Edna. "On Presumption." *Journal of Philosophy,* 80 (1983): 143–63.

Ullmann-Margalit, Edna, and Avisha Margalit. "Analyticity by Way of Presumption." *Canadian Journal of Philosophy,* 12 (1982): 435–52.

Underwood, Barbara D. "The Thumb on the Scales of Justice: Burdens of Persuasion in Criminal Cases." *Yale Law Journal,* 86 (1977): 1199–348.

U.S. Atomic Energy Commission [U.S. Nuclear Regulatory Commission]. *An Assessment of Accident Risks in U.S. Commercial Nuclear Power Plants.* Washington, D.C.: U.S. Government Printing Office, 1974.

U.S. Food and Drug Administration. "Chemical Compounds in Food-processing Animals. Criteria and Procedures for Evaluating Assays of Carcinogenic Residues." Washington, D. C.: U.S. Government Printing Office, March 20, 1979; 44 *Federal Register,* 17060–114.

Vollmer, H. M., and D. L. Mills (eds.,). *Professionalization.* Englewood Cliffs: Prentice Hall, 1966.

Walters, R. S. "Laws of Science and Lawlike Statements." In *Encyclopedia of Philosophy*, Vol. IV edited by P. Edwards, pp. 410–14. New York: Macmillan, 1967.

Walton, Douglas N. "Burden of Proof." *Argumentation*, 2 (1988): 233–54.

Walton, Douglas N. *Informal Logic*. Cambridge: Cambridge University Press, 1989.

Walton, Douglas N. *Argumentation Schemes for Presumptive Reasoning*. Mahwah, N.J.: Lawrence Erlbaum, 1996.

Walton, Douglas N. *Plausible Argument in Everyday Conversation*. Albany: State University of New York Press, 1992.

Walton, Douglas N. *Arguments from Ignorance*. University Park, Penn.: Pennsylvania State University Press, 1995).

Ward, G., and L. Harn (eds.). *Handbook of Pragmatics*. Oxford: Basil Blackwell, 2003.

Whately, Richard. *Elements of Logic*. New York: William Jackson, 1836.

Whately, Richard. *Elements of Rhetoric*. London and Oxford: John Murry and J. F. Parker, 1828.

White, A. R. "Coherence Theory of Truth." In *Encyclopedia of Philosophy*, edited by P. Edwards 2 (1967): 130–3.

Wigmore, John Henry. *A Treatise on the Anglo-American System of Evidence in Trials at Common Law*, Vol. 10 (Boston: Little, Brown, 1904–1905; 3rd ed., 1940.

Wigmore, John Henry. *The Principles of Judicial Proof*. Boston, 1913; with numerous later editions.

Wigmore, John Henry. *Evidence in Trials at Common Law*, revised by T. Chadbonn. Boston: Little, Brown, 1981.

Willard, Charles A. *Theory of Argumentation*. Tuscaloosa: University of Alabama Press, 1981.

Index of Names